Preface

Never before has there been such a popular interest in and concern for tropical rain forests. The destruction of the world's richest biome has made good copy for newspapers and learned periodicals alike. In the last twenty years there has been an upsurge in tropical studies of all kinds. To be invited to write a book as an introductory text for undergraduates therefore presents a daunting task when so much is being investigated, and when ideas and hypotheses are being promulgated in a race with the saws and fires that are destroying the very object of study. Over the last seven years, I have been privileged to lecture on aspects of the rain forest to botanists, agricultural and forest scientists and geographers. In a book as short as this, as in a series of lectures, only pointers to further study can be given. Furthermore, such a short text, as in lectures, is likely to reflect the author's main interests and this book is no exception. It is impossible here to do justice to the zoological literature, and I have deliberately dwelt on the trees and other plants that make up the structure of the forests in which the animals live. Nevertheless, the modern forest cannot exist without animals, and I have drawn attention to those interactions which have received recent investigation and interest. My principal aim, however, has been to show the importance of change as well as diversity in the rain forest and to try to indicate how *Homo sapiens* and his habits are involved in this.

The greatest synthesis on tropical rain forest yet published is by P. W. Richards (*The Tropical Rain Forest*, Cambridge University Press, 1952). All subsequent textbooks have relied heavily on this and, although it has not yet been revised, it is still a most valuable source-book and should be consulted by the serious student who wishes to take the subject further. A more recent compilation is a UNESCO publication with many contributing authors: *Tropical Forest Ecosystems—A State of Knowledge Report*, prepared by UNESCO, UNEP, FAO (Paris, 1978), which is wider-ranging with much more stress on human biology and economics, and, although rather indigestible, a valuable guide to the more recent literature. Regional works include, pre-eminently, T. C. Whitmore's magnificent *Tropical Rain Forests of the Far East* (Clarendon Press, 1975), which is superbly illustrated and of which a second edition is in preparation. Other valuable books with different slants are K. A. Longman's and J. Jeník's *Tropical Forest and its Environment* (Longman, 1974) which is rich in physiology; J. R. Flenley's *Equatorial Rain Forest: a Geological History* (Butterworth, 1979); and F. Hallé's, R. A. A. Oldeman's and P. B. Tomlinson's *Tropical Trees and Forests: An Architectural Analysis* (Springer, 1978), with a morphological flavour; while a symposium volume edited by P. B. Tomlinson and M. H. Zimmermann, *Tropical Trees as Living Systems* (Cambridge University Press, 1978), contains much valuable material. All these will repay study, for only a superficial rendering of the principal areas of the subject can be made in a book intended to be an introduction, as is the present one. I have indicated, by numbers in parentheses, references to striking or original ideas or facts in these texts and in original research papers, for those who wish to follow up particular points. These references are listed chapter by chapter at the end of the book.

I am painfully aware that most undergraduates know little of tropical plants and animals, while the grounding in the basics of botany and zoology, which could be relied on until fairly recently as having been taught at school, is often lacking, too, largely through the cyclical fashion of curricula. Unfamiliar tree and other plant names in Latin are inevitably a hurdle to many. *Flowering Plants of the World*, edited by V. H. Heywood (Oxford University Press, 1978), and J. C. Willis's *Dictionary of the Flowering Plants and Ferns* (Cambridge University Press) in its various editions (the earlier ones have more general information) should put many of them into context and provide some further facts about their distribution, uses and so on. Finally, an unsurpassed general text which looks at plants and their involvements with animals from a tropical angle is E. J. H. Corner's *The Life of Plants* (Weidenfeld and Nicolson, 1964, with recent reprints and paper editions), which, unlike most textbooks, is not only a sparkling account to be read continuously from cover to cover, but is also the nearest that any modern biological work I know comes to literature.

TERTIARY LEVEL BIOLOGY

Tropical Rain Forest Ecology

D. J. MABBERLEY, M.A., D.Phil.

Lecturer in Plant Ecology
University of Oxford

Blackie

Glasgow and London

Distributed in the USA by
Chapman and Hall
New York

Blackie & Son Limited
Bishopbriggs, Glasgow G64 2NZ

Furnival House, 14–18 High Holborn, London WC1V 6BX

Distributed in the USA by
Chapman and Hall
in association with Methuen, Inc.
733 Third Avenue, New York, N.Y. 10017

British Library Cataloguing in Publication Data

Mabberley, D. J.
    Tropical rain forest ecology.
    1. Jungle ecology
    I. Title
    574.5′2642′0913   QH541.5.J8

ISBN 0-216-91510-4
ISBN 0-216-91509-0 Pbk

For the USA, International Standard Book Numbers are
0-412-00431-3
0-412-00441-0 Pbk

Filmset by Advanced Filmsetters (Glasgow) Ltd
Printed in Britain by Bell & Bain Ltd.

Tropical Rain Forest Ecology

T!

14

TERTIARY LEVEL BIOLOGY

A series covering selected areas of biology at advanced undergraduate level. While designed specifically for course options at this level within Universities and Polytechnics, the series will be of great value to specialists and research workers in other fields who require a knowledge of the essentials of a subject.

I am indebted to many people for their encouragement and help in the production of this book but would like to record specifically the inspiration I have received from Gary S. Hartshorn. My greatest debt, however, is undoubtedly that to G. E. O. Miles (1922–1964), headmaster, who fostered my earliest aspirations in science: this book is dedicated to his memory.

D.J.M.
Wadham College, Oxford

Contents

CHAPTER ONE

THE TROPICAL RAIN FOREST

A great deal of Botany is based on herbarium sheets, collecting tubes, microscope slides, wood-blocks, and petri dishes. These are little things which carry only little plants or bits of the big. We start with *Ranunculus* or *Capsella* and go down the scale to *Chlamydomonas*, *Spirogyra*, *Fucus* (which is a little out of the way, and getting unmanageable), *Agaricus*, *Funaria* and *Nephrodium*. We learn of trees from twigs, sporophylls and stained preparations. We are led away by chromosomes, *Neurospora*, subspecies, pollen grains, and ultrastructure. We research in grassland, heath, plantations, sea-shore, desert, and savannah. And, if we have the luck to reach the tropical forest, the immensity is baffling: we collect all the common little things which have been collected there before, because there is no time for the big. So botany has been compounded from its myriad particles, its manageable objects, and its easily presentable aspects: the pursuit is minuter. The cry is in the cities. The principles of plant-life can be demonstrated in dishes, flasks, pots, frames and borders. The graduation is from universities where academic distinction lies. Our grandfathers went to the backwoods to find out: our benches are stacked with costly instruments, that detain us. The axe and the pocket-lens, the flora and the systematic eye are recreations for a holiday. The struggle for existence is common sense, natural selection just a sieve through which the smaller pass. Oh, what a desert the cities are making of our science! Turn with me, for a moment, to the great depots of plant life in the tropical forests, and see the effect. The little flowers and fruits are hoist on big trees: and how do little *Ranunculus* and *Alisma*, *Helianthus* and *Poa*, *Funaria* and *Nephrodium* compete with them? (E. J. H. Corner, 'On thinking big', *Phytomorphology*, **17** (1967) 24).

The diverse and rich flora and fauna of the tropics have bewildered, overwhelmed and humbled those trained in the biologically impoverished temperate regions. Such an experience is essential for those who wish to pursue tropical studies, and has been that of all the great traveller-naturalists such as Henry Walter Bates and Alfred Russel Wallace (1) in the last century. Long before them, the pioneering Dutchman, Georg Everard Rumpf, set down the more remarkable of the plants of the tiny

1

island of Ambon in the Moluccas, and his fellow countryman, Hendrik van Rheede tot Draakenstein, supervised the first major work to bring a tropical flora to the notice of Europeans. This was the monumental Flora of part of India in twelve folio volumes, the *Hortus Indicus Malabaricus* (1678–1702). These works, like the chain of botanic gardens and other research institutes established later, were the by-products of European colonial expansion. And, indeed, the first indication of the riches of the tropics had come from similar colonial ambition, for Alexander the Great, having defeated the Persian King Darius in 331 BC, had pushed on over the Khyber Pass to the Punjab of India, so that the Indus became the eastern boundary of his extended Asiatic empire. Though the extent of the enormous enterprise was shortlived, the culture and natural history of India was forever thereafter linked to that of the western world. Findings from his invasion were incorporated in Theophrastus's influential *Enquiry into Plants*: the banana, the mango and *jak* fruit (Fig. 13), cotton and mangroves, the astonishing trees living in the sea, and the banyan (*Ficus benghalensis*), putting out aerial roots, which undermined the ancients' view of what roots did.

1.1 A tropical origin for ecology?

Today, with an increasingly less parochial view of biology, scientists are turning more and more to the tropics as a means of understanding ecological and evolutionary problems set in a temperate context. Such an approach has led to new insights and concepts readily applied in ecology. But it is true to say that this apparently recent change of heart or emphasis is no new departure peculiar to 'modern' biology, for much of the advance in biological science in the last century derived from tropical experience. In the eighteenth century, it had been widely believed that, though the tropics had a number of peculiar organisms, they were not particularly rich in species, at least in species of plant. Indeed, Linnaeus himself seems to have believed that the tropical flora was rather homogeneous and limited. This attitude may well have reflected the collections of pantropical weeds around settlements, and of the widespread littoral species readily accessible to travellers and brought back to Europe. Access to the canopy of rain forest was rarely obtained and such familiar tropical phenomena as cauliflory, the bearing of flowers on the trunks of trees, so little understood that a mahogany relation with cauliflorous flowers was thought to be a parasite by Linnaeus's pupil Osbeck, who named it *Melia parasitica*, the *Dysoxylum parasiticum* of today. More extensive travelling and the penetration of the continents led to a discarding of these ideas and, by the turn of the nineteenth century, attitudes were changing rapidly, partly due, at least, to advances in attempts to put some geographical order into the hordes of plants and animals being brought back to Europe.

Nonetheless, most classical ecological studies have been carried out in the more accessible north temperate zone and it is perhaps surprising to learn that it can be convincingly argued that the scientific study of what we now call ecology began in the tropics of South America (2). Early ideas on plant distribution were brought together following two early nineteenth-century expeditions to the tropics: Alexander von Humboldt climbing the Ecuadorean volcano, Mount Chimborazo (6300 m and, at the time, thought to be the world's highest peak) and noting the correlation between climate and vegetation type as he ascended, and Robert Brown, on Matthew Flinders's voyage to Australia, preparing an early phyto-geographical account of that continent and, later, of tropical Africa. These two pioneers were mutual admirers and corresponded, von Humboldt going on to produce influential treatises, the biogeographical ideas in which were taken up by zoologists, who established faunal provinces similar to the world schemes of vegetation types built on the work of von Humboldt and Brown. It must be remembered that it was the tropical environment that is alleged to have triggered both Charles Darwin and Wallace to formulate their converging views on the mode of evolution by natural selection, where Darwin stressed the biotic relationships while Wallace stressed the physical environment in essentially ecologically-based theories of evolution.

It is true that, as in much of science, some of these ideas were not altogether new, for the seventeenth-century Dutch microscopist, Antony van Leeuwenhoek, developed the idea of the importance of food chains, and, from his observations of the shellfishes in Dutch canals, came to some idea of competition between organisms, while in the following century, Count Buffon was groping towards the concept of what is now termed succession. Nonetheless, these figures did not, in these areas of inquiry, affect the mainstream of scientific thought as it was passed on to the nineteenth century. Only then was the scientific world receptive and the key figure is held to have been Eugen Warming, a Dane who spent three years writing what would now be considered an ecological survey, an account of the forest around the Brazilian village of Lagoa Santa. He returned to Europe to give courses in ecology in the University of Copenhagen and wrote the first textbook specifically devoted to ecology (1895), but because, in 1898, A. F. W. Schimper published his *Pflanzen-*

geographie auf physiologischer Grundlage, a book to become a standard
text in English as well as German, leaning heavily on Warming's work
though without even a footnote to acknowledge it, Warming's pioneering
contribution has been largely overlooked.

1.2   Tropical forests

It was Schimper who coined the term *tropische Regenwald*, tropical rain
forest, and contrasted it with monsoon forest which was more or less
leafless during the dry season, especially towards the end. His definition of
rain forest was 'evergreen, hygrophilous in character, at least 30 m high,
rich in thick-stemmed lianes, and in woody as well as herbaceous epiphytes'. Monsoon forest was lower generally and, though rich in woody
lianes and herbaceous epiphytes, poor in woody epiphytes. Lianes are
woody 'climbers', which are often carried up into the canopy by maturing
trees and are very poorly represented in temperate countries. For example,
in the British Isles, the only species are ivy (*Hedera helix*, Araliaceae), old
man's beard (*Clematis vitalba*, Ranunculaceae) and honeysuckle (*Lonicera
periclymenum*, Caprifoliaceae), whereas 170 species have been recorded
from one tiny island in the Panama Canal. Epiphytes are plants living
perched on, but not necessarily deriving sustenance from, other plants. In
temperate countries, such plants, excluding marine and other aquatic
forms and parasites, are generally herbaceous and small, chiefly bryophytes,
lichens and algae.

The term 'rain forest' has been so long established in the literature that
it is retained in the broad sense here. Although rain forest is in general
associated with heavy rainfall, it embraces certain riparian forests in
seasonal climates. Again, in cool everwet climates, there are temperate rain
forests, as along the Pacific coast of North America for example. The
humid lowland tropics account for less than a third of the tropical land
surface (3), which has deserts, savannas and grasslands as well as montane
vegetation types. In attempts to assess the present-day status of forests in
the tropics, the term 'tropical moist forest' (4) has become current and
much of the work discussed in this book has been carried out in vegetation
covered by this term, rather than in rain forest in the narrow sense. Myers
has defined it as 'evergreen or partly evergreen in areas receiving not less
than 100 mm of precipitation in any month for two out of three years, with
mean annual temperature of more than 24° C and frost free'. It usually lies
below 1300 m but, according to Myers, does not reach above 750 m in
south-east Asia, and includes cloud forest, riparian forest, swamp and bog

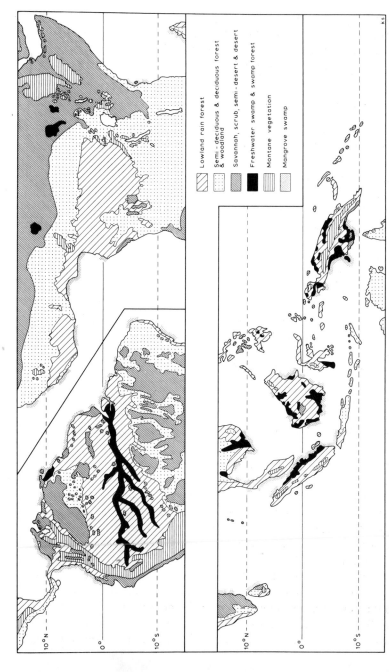

Figure 1 Tropical vegetation types. Reproduced with permission from J. R. Flenley, *Equatorial Rain Forest: a Geological History* (Butterworth, 1979). Tropical lowland rain forest represents the major part of tropical moist forests, which in 1976 covered some 935 million ha, the size of the United States. This is 71 % of the total area of closed tropical forest and almost 30 % of all the world's forests. 472 million ha were in South America, centred on the basins of the Amazon and Orinoco, 187 million ha in Asia, largely Malesia, and 175 million ha in Central Africa with an extension to Sierra Leone.

Lowland rain forest

Semi - deciduous & deciduous forest & woodland

Savannah, scrub, semi - desert & desert

Freshwater swamp & swamp forest

Montane vegetation

Mangrove swamp

forest and the wetter end of the lowland seasonal forest as well as what is regarded as rain forest in the narrow sense. The difficulty of drawing up worldwide definitions led Myers to consider the absence of seasonality as more critical than overall precipitation. For example, much of Latin America has more than 4000 mm of precipitation per annum, a figure rare in Asia and almost unknown in Africa where 1500 mm is often considered the minimum to support rain forest, while in Latin America this is the midpoint for the maintenance of tropical dry forests.

Such forests are not precisely restricted to the tropics in that they extend to 28° N in southern China, though they are largely cleared from there, also into Mexico and southwards down the east slopes of Madagascar, the southern end of the coastal strip of Brazilian rain forest and the eastern coast of Australia. At these extremes, it differs somewhat and is often referred to as subtropical rain forest. In turn this grades into subtemperate and temperate rain forests like those, for example, in Japan and New Zealand. In the north island of New Zealand at 34–47° S, the rain forests have conspicuous woody epiphytes and even a strangling *Metrosideros* (Myrtaceae), reminiscent of the strangling figs (see section 5.2.2) of the tropical forests (5). At the edges of its distribution or under stressful climatic conditions, rain forest merges into semi-evergreen rain forest, a belt lying between the evergreen and moist deciduous forests. The more seasonal of the subtropical rain forests are prone to conflagration at the hands of man or from lightning and have been largely degraded to open woodlands and savanna, notably in Burma and Thailand and much of Africa but such are more rarely encountered in South America. On the coasts, the mangrove swamps become lower in stature the further they grow from the equator and eventually pass into the saltmarsh vegetation familiar in temperate regions.

In this biome are several million species of organisms, of which fewer than half a million even have a Latin name (4), and a minute fraction of them are at all understood in terms of their ecology or even distribution. Although covering only 6 % of the world's surface, the forest contains about half the earth's total of animal and plant species, including, for example, some 70–75 % of all known arthropods. The most extensive tracts of forest are those in the Americas: the forests of the eastern Andes, the Amazon basin and the Caribbean as a whole account for about a sixth of the total non-coniferous forest in the world. It is exceedingly difficult to estimate the potential and actual areas covered by the world's tropical rain forest but it has been calculated from aerial surveys, satellite photographs and other methods that some 16 million km^2 is potentially rain-forest land but that today there is about 9–11 million km^2. This is 71 % of the total area of closed tropical forest and almost 30 % of all the world's forest. In the mid-1970s this was declining at the rate of some 11 000 km^2 per annum and it was estimated that some 37 % had been lost in Latin America, 41.6 % from Asia and 51.6 % from Africa, while more recently it has been estimated that over half of the world's rain forest has gone. The rate of forest removal today is variously estimated at between 11 and 40 ha *per*

Table 1 Numbers of individuals and species of trees with a diameter at breast height of 10 cm and over in mixed tropical rain forest

	Plot size, ha (approx.)	No. of trees per ha	No. of species on plot*
Borneo, Andalau For. Res.			
Ridge	2.0	740	199 (118)
Valley bottom	2.0	640	219 (129)
Sepilok For. Res.			
Ridge forest	2.0	667	198 (144)
Malay Peninsula, Bukit Lagong For. Res.			
Hill forest	2.0	559	251
Sungai Menyala For. Res.			
Probably alluvium forest	1.6	489	197
New Guinea			
Hill forest	0.8	652	122
	0.8	691	147
	0.8	526	145
Forest on flat river terrace and gentle foot slope	0.8	430	116
Cameroon, Southern Bakundu For. Res.	1.5	368	109
Nigeria			
Okomu For. Res.	18.5	451	170
Okomu For. Res.	1.5	390	70
Omo For. Res.	1.5	521	42
Guyana			
Moraballi Creek	1.5	432	91
Panama, Barro Colorado Is.	1.5	489	—
Surinam			
Plot 5, Coesewijne Ri.	1.0	—	116 (106)
Plot 1, Mapane Cr.	3.0	—	168 (108)

* Figures in parentheses represent approximate numbers of species on 0.8 ha gauged from available species/area curves. (From K. Paijmans (ed.) *New Guinea Vegetation*, CSIRO & ANU Press, Canberra, 1976, p. 71).

minute. The richness of some of the forests can be gauged from the statistics from the Malay Peninsula which is estimated to have 7900 plant species in *c.* 1500 genera in an area half the size of Britain (which has some 1430 species in 620 genera). Though the rain forests of Fiji may be as poor as those of the richest North American forests, the oft-cited species-rich *fynbos* vegetation of South Africa is comparable in diversity to the poorest rain-forest samples. In the richest tracts of rain forest, as in south-east Asia, Amazonia (Manaus area), Peru and Costa Rica, there may be more than 150 species of tree with a diameter greater than 15 cm in each hectare.

Such forests are marked by certain features besides those in Schimper's definition. They are notable for the strangling habit most familiar in the pantropical *Ficus* (Moraceae), but also in *Clusia* (Guttiferae, Neotropics) and *Wightia* (Scrophulariaceae, Indomalesia); there is a poverty of leaf-litter, reflecting a rapid decomposition rate and speedy recycling of nutrients (a tree may disappear completely five years after falling, through the action of fungi and termites); the involvement of animals in herbivory, pollination and dispersal is various and more marked than in most other vegetation types, with a consequent range of flower and fruit presentation much greater than in temperate zones; there is a wide range of tree-form, both in general *bauplan* and in relative massiveness of leaves, buds and twigs; and there is a marked parallelism between families in the range of response to the ecological opportunities arising from the formation of gaps in the forest through the fall of trees.

On a world scale it is difficult to gauge floristic richness in rain forests. Should the generic diversity or family diversity be considered more important than the number of species? A further complication in using the latter criterion is the man-made one, for it has been argued that recent workers on the tropical Asiatic flora have had a wider species concept than, say, many of those working in the Neotropics. Nevertheless, it is generally held that some of the richest forests are those in south-east Asia, the wettest forests of which correspond to the ombrophilous forest (or rain forest in the narrow sense) of earlier classifications. These are remarkable for the abundance and diversity of one particular family which is of enormous commercial importance, the Dipterocarpaceae. Malaya alone has nine genera and 155 (127 endemic) species. Such forests in Sarawak and Brunei in Borneo have 2000 species of tree with a diameter greater than 10 cm. This compares with a figure of 849 in the heath forest and 234 in the peat-swamp forest, two forest types to be considered below, in the same island. Compared with these rich forests, those in the same region with an annual water stress of at least a few weeks' duration are poorer and differ in a number of features, although they are considered here under the umbrella of tropical rain forest (6). These would include the extension down the east coast of Australia, and parts of the Indian and Indo-Chinese rain forests, also the Philippines, Lesser Sunda Islands and parts of New Guinea. Such forest is probably the most extensive of all rain-forest formations in much of central Amazonia and the Caribbean and probably corresponds to the moister of the African rain forests. In it, there is a greater tendency for a marked gregariousness of trees while deciduous trees may make up to a third of the taller tree species. The bark tends to be thicker and rougher in these tree species, and cauliflory and ramiflory, the bearing of the flowers on the branches, is rarer. The canopy height is somewhat lower and there are fewer large lianes, while it is more easily destroyed by fire and thus replaced by grassland.

1.3 Some misconceptions

Possibly springing from boys' adventure books of the nineteenth century and from the more purple passages of over-enthusiastic travelogues of the period, is the idea that tropical rain forest is dark, steamy and impenetrable, overrun with snakes and crawling with poisonous insects and other dangers. Much of this comes from a superficial knowledge of the tangle of secondary forests or forest along river-edges. Such places were the first to be encountered by travellers and, indeed, are difficult to penetrate. Furthermore, hacking a path through them is likely to disturb animals, some of which at least may react less than pleasantly to the destruction of their habitat. Within the forest proper, however, it is generally rather easy to move about without cutting a path and it is rarely so wet as to make progress difficult. It may be dark here and there but the mosaic pattern of regenerating forest and treefalls and the movement of sunflecks belie the myth of overall dismalness. It is often cooler than cleared land outside, although the absence of a breeze may make human beings insensitive to this.

There are diurnal fluctuations in temperature, so conditions cannot be described as uniform, and spatially there are many differences in physical features between the canopy of the forest and at ground level, near the bases of trees and away from them. Furthermore, as noted above, there is a marked seasonality in many areas and in most regions 'rainy' or 'dry' seasons are readily recognizable and generally rather predictable. The myth of constant growing conditions is often linked with that of constant growth, but few plants grow continuously and few animals breed continuously. As far as the trees are concerned, most have an obvious flushing period and some have bud-scales like those of temperate trees. Another widely-held misconception is that the forest resembles some flower-stuffed greenhouse. Such ideas derive from the magnificent displays in conservatories and botanical garden hothouses in temperate countries on the one hand and from the brightly-coloured plantings seen in tropical cities and their gardens on the other. The massing of cosseted flowering specimens in serried pots and the gaudy pantropical garden flora contrast markedly with the monotonous green within the forest. In general, spectacular flowering occurs only at canopy level, though occasional brilliant cauliflorous trees provide beautiful exceptions.

Perhaps more serious is the belief, still surprisingly widely held, that the forest stands on potentially good agricultural land. In temperate countries this is often so, as in Britain where the limewoods (*Tilia cordata*) were probably the first to disappear at the hand of man, for they stood on the best land in terms of agriculture as practised then. In the tropics, good agricultural land is to be found but much forest stands on poor land and its removal may lead to irreparable degradation of the soil. This point will be returned to later, as will be the variable physical features of the tropical rain forest environment.

An increasing unfamiliarity with forest, associated with greater sophistication of urban living, may lead to the forest being considered backward, despicable, even to be feared and, at least, not agreeable. Embedded in some of the more horrific fairy tales of Europe is such a fear of the forest with its darkness, unknowns, ogres and beasts. Today, the urbanized tropical inhabitant may have little time for the 'primitive' and 'backward' forest people and their habitat, their knowledge of how to live in and manipulate the forest in terms of gathering, hunting and shifting cultivation. Rather, they may mimic the early European colonists with disastrous consequences.

A final misconception is one due largely, it appears, to the wishful thinking of biologists themselves, though possibly it represents a higher sentiment, namely the desire to work in primeval, original, virgin, untouched, undisturbed or primary forest. What is primary forest? Secondary forest deriving from the revegetation of completely cleared tracts of land can persist for a very long time. Around the great temples of Angkor (Kampuchea), forest cleared 600 years ago and since recolonized still does not resemble fully 'undisturbed' forest patches, and indeed it has been estimated that at least a thousand years may be required (7). Forests long considered primary are now known to have archaeological remains, arguing wholesale clearance in historical time. Networks of canals more than a thousand years old have been seen as a grid pattern by Synthetic Aperture Radar, possibly indicating raised field cultivation of maize and cocoa in Maya times in areas now covered by the Guatemalan rain forest (8). In the Petén of that country and the Yucatán of Mexico, present-day abundance of *Swietenia macrophylla* (mahogany, Meliaceae), *Achras zapota* (chicle, Sapotaceae) and *Brosimum alicastrum* (ramon, Moraceae) is thought to reflect the cultural practices of that civilization, where these species were encouraged to regenerate. There is now plenty of evidence of European archaeological remains, not to speak of aboriginal settlements in Central and South America, and it is estimated that since 1825 (4), the forest of Venezuela increased in area from 21 % of its original range to 45 % in 1950. Are such forests 'restored' or of a new type? How can they be recognized when there is no absolute yardstick for comparison? There is a long history of settlement in West Africa and Central America and it could be argued that rain forests there represent 'old secondary' rather than 'primary' forests typical of territories like Borneo but even those have long been influenced by man, as naturalized fruit trees and discoveries of medieval Chinese pottery indicate. In short, most forests are probably 'disturbed' but some are more disturbed than others.

1.4 The tropical rain forest in a wider context

1.4.1 *Floristics*

Certain groups of plants familiar to the biologist of the temperate zones are also well-represented in the tropics. Compositae, for example, are common there, though many of their number in forest vegetation are trees and shrubs. Euphorbiaceae and Leguminosae have similar patterns while, in the monocotyledons, Gramineae, Liliaceae and Orchidaceae (largely epiphytic in the tropics) are also widespread. Rubiaceae, represented by herbs in temperate regions, are predominantly woody in the tropics. Indeed, many of the families exclusively tropical in distribution are exclusively woody. Many genera of the temperate regions, after which families have been named, turn out to be very atypical, such as *Lythrum*, *Polygala*, *Verbena* and *Urtica*, which are mostly herbs in Europe, while their relations in the tropics are largely woody. Conversely, in the tropics there are woody members of widespread and predominantly herbaceous temperate families such as *Bocconia*, a woody poppy from South America, and the 'giant' *Lobelia* species (Campanulaceae) of the African, American and Pacific tropics.

Studies of the tropical flora lead to the blurring of the clearcut differences between families recognized first from their temperate representatives. Thus Araliaceae and Umbelliferae have now been merged by some and many monocotyledon lily allies brought together in an enlarged Liliaceae including Amaryllidaceae. The differences between the figs (Moraceae), the elms (Ulmaceae) and the nettles (Urticaceae) are slight indeed as are those between Scrophulariaceae and Bignoniaceae, to take another example.

If the flora of a temperate country, Great Britain for example, is analysed we find it has an interesting relation to that of the tropics. The native British angiosperms are considered to belong to some 43 orders, all of which are represented in tropical regions. Furthermore, with the exception of aquatics, parasites and insectivorous plants, they are all represented by woody, sometimes exclusively woody, species there. The only striking exceptions are the Centrospermae, which thrive in open dry habitats and are scarcely woody anywhere except in salt deserts, the Cucurbitales, which are tender forest-scramblers and lianes, represented by *Bryonia* alone, the sea-pinks (Plumbaginaceae), the plantains (Plantaginaceae), the orchids, sedges and grasses, although it must be pointed out that there are dendroid forms of all of these in the tropics or subtropics. Some of the British plants take on an extra interest when they are seen as outposts of large tropical families: such are the black bryony, *Tamus communis* (Dioscoreaceae, yams), ivy in the almost exclusively tropical Araliaceae, the naturalized periwinkles, *Vinca* (Apocynaceae), as well as the white bryony, *Bryonia*.

1.4.2 *Numbers of species*

It is well known that the tropics harbour an enormous number of plant species and such samples (Table 1) as the 23 ha of West Malaysian rain forest with 375 species of tree (in 139 genera in 52 families) with a diameter greater than 91 cm are a staple of textbooks, but in the species-rich *Festuca* turf of the chalklands of Britain up to 40 or 45 species of angiosperms and bryophytes have been recorded in one square metre. With such differences in scale, comparisons are rather pointless, but the comparison of species numbers within large genera in vegetation types is perhaps more interesting. Excluding the hordes of apomictic clones of *Hieracium* and *Taraxacum* in the British flora, the largest genus by far is *Carex* with 75 species, which compares favourably with the 66 found in the whole of Malesia, but such statistics pale into insignificance when the estimated numbers of tropical species of *Piper* (2000), *Solanum* (1500) or *Vernonia* (1000) are considered. Nevertheless, such enormous genera as *Astragalus* (2000 spp.) and *Silene* (500 spp.) are largely temperate and the extraordinary diversity of the southern African *Erica, Aspalathus* and *Helichrysum* is outside the tropics. Furthermore, there are some very species-poor forest types in the tropics: mangroves have, at best, 25 tree species, often many fewer, while tropical deserts have a small number of woody species and lack the large ephemeral flora of the temperate deserts. In wet places too, species diversity may be low, as in the papyrus swamps of northern Uganda. These do not appear to be unstable and it is perhaps as instructive to ponder why such species-poor tropical ecosystems are not subject to an enormous grazing pressure from animals as it is to ask why rain forests at their richest are so diverse (9).

1.4.3   The global interest

For biologists, the riches of the tropics are a great attraction. For other people in temperate countries, the rain forest represents a large resource, 50 % of the earth's standing timber, and, it has been estimated, some 75 % of the potential production of wood products. It is an enormous gene pool resource and the source of a wide range of products, often unrecognized in the slick retailing of temperate countries, from teabags (from the leaf sheath of a banana originating in the Philippines) to Brazil nuts, the only tropical food crop marketed in Europe and collected from the forest rather than cultivated. There are drugs, gums and other extractives, tropical fruits and other foods, but it is timber that is the largest resource at present exploited with the utility timbers such as teak and ramin (*Gonystylus bancanus* from the peat-swamp forests of Borneo and widely used in mouldings), merantis and their allies with a wide range of uses including plywood (*Shorea* spp., Dipterocarpaceae of Malesia) and luxury timbers such as the mahoganies and peroba (*Paratecoma peroba*, Bignoniaceae, Brazil). To tropical peoples, the forest may represent productivity on otherwise useless sites, especially erodable or creep sites or on deep deposits of peat, and to many it is home.

CHAPTER TWO

THE CHANGING PHYSICAL SETTING

An extension of the myth of the 'undisturbed' forest is the idea that rain forests are static and unchanging, that for a very long time they have been as they are today. It has been argued that rain forests are museums of period pieces of botany and zoology, even though the arrays of closely related species there might indicate rapidly evolving groups of organisms. That the forests, even without man, have been changing is evident from the geological history and that they are in a constant state of turmoil comes from modern ecological work, which is the subject of Chapter 4. Here, the ancient history of rain forest is discussed.

2.1   Continental drift

It has been established that the land masses of the earth are moving with respect to one another through the forces of sea-floor spreading and detailed maps of the relative position of continents at different times are being drawn up with increasing precision (1). At the same time as the continents were fragmenting in the Cretaceous, the angiosperms and their associated animals which have given rise to the modern flowering plant forest were evolving. Long before, there may have been forests in the Devonian, but the best known, through abundant fossils, are the coal-swamp forests of the Upper Carboniferous of Europe and North America, which were then in the equatorial tropics. These trees exhibited a wide range of form seen in modern but unrelated plants, where much of this range is still restricted to tropical regions. There were massive unbranched ferns with big buds and leaves (pachycaul), like modern tree ferns, and the oldest coniferoid gymnosperms had stilt-roots and a combination of anatomical features today seen only in some mangrove trees. These all disappeared with the increasing aridity of the Permian. The next tropical forests were of conifers, which are represented today by, among others, the enormous *Araucaria* species of New Guinea and New Caledonia, and it was these forests which the angiosperms largely replaced in the Cretaceous.

There are many tropical pollen sequences from Cretaceous angiosperms but leaf floras are almost unknown and reconstructions of the takeover have been derived from modern ecology. The most inviting picture has been painted by Ashton (2) where the *Araucaria* forest with ferns in the shade beneath has cycads and Caytoniales on the open fringes, along ridges and in swampy plains. The opportunities in ecological terms of occupying the gap phase, the holes made in the forest by falling trees, may have selected the fast-growing opportunist tree almost unknown outside the angiosperms. These protoangiosperms may thus have crowded out the gymnosperm seedlings and, as a group, radiated to become climax trees as well. The angiosperms in this reconstruction are seen as a basically tropical group, initially poorly adapted to colder climates. The closing of the carpel, and hence the distinctness of the angiosperms as a group, is seen as an adaptation to protection from herbivory rather than a protection against desiccation, for which such a device would have been 'pre-adapted' (3).

During the Cretaceous, when the angiosperms were diverging from their seed-fern allies, the apparently temporarily consolidated world-continent, Pangaea, was breaking up into several areas of continental crust. The largest piece became Antarctica and Australasia, the smallest India and Madagascar. The sea penetrated the rift between Africa and South America while, by the Upper Cretaceous, Madagascar was separating from India. At this time, the chalk was being deposited in enormous volumes over much of Europe as the world underwent its greatest inundation since the Ordovician. It has been estimated that 40 % of the continents were covered, i.e. only 18 % of the world's surface was land, though estimates of the increase in sea depth vary from 350 m to 650 m. Such features as a trans-Saharan seaway allowed migration of marine faunas, but the evidence from the Pacific region rather supports the view that sea-levels there were rather similar to those of today. Much of tropical South America was inundated. In Australia a great inland sea appears to have shrunk in this period, but New Zealand seems to have been scarcely affected as it split off from Australia.

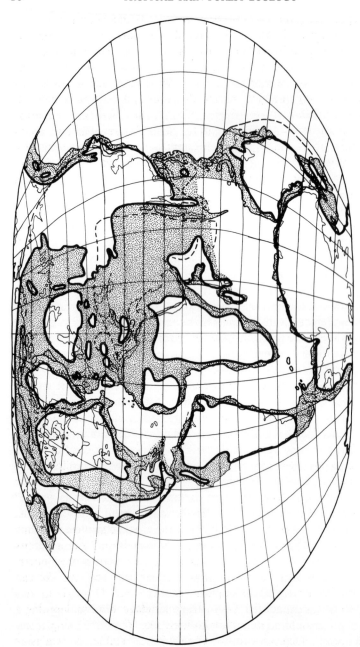

Figure 2 World geography during the Upper Cretaceous, 90–80 million years ago, on a base map reconstructed on a globe 90% of the present earth diameter. Redrawn from H. G. Owen in M. K. Howarth in L. R. M. Cocks (ed.), *The Evolving Earth* (British Museum (Natural History) and Cambridge University Press, 1981). The bold lines indicate coastlines in the Cretaceous.

By the beginning of the Tertiary (65 m years ago), the Atlantic was 75 % of its present width while Africa was a few degrees further south than it is today and India straddled the equator as an island. The sea level had fallen, though the cause is not yet understood, and it was to rise again, but never to the levels of the Cretaceous. The Amazon basin, however, was a site of continental and not marine deposition. The oceans between the southern and northern continents allowed the migration of marine organisms, but the crossing from one to the other by terrestrial ones could only have been by 'island hopping' on temporarily unsubmerged blocks. It has been suggested that in the early Tertiary the sea-grasses spread, leading in turn to faunal spread and diversification, as well as affecting sediment patterns. In the Eocene, the well-known London Clay Flora was growing in the Thames Valley and included many plants which, if they existed now, would be placed in a wide range of temperate and tropical groups, many of them of very restricted distribution. It has been said that, in the Tertiary, tropical and subtropical plants could live further from the equator than they do today, while others have argued that the London Clay Flora has a large drift component of material swept into it from further south. It must be remembered that even modern forests as far south as New Zealand still have a flora of mixed temperate and tropical types, though the presence in the deposit of the characteristic fruits of the taxonomically isolated palm, *Nypa*, now known only from the mangroves of tropical Asia and the western Pacific, is not readily explained away. The London Clay Flora is very different from the pollen records of the tropics at this period and pollens are known from south-east Asia, which if they were found in modern plants, would be referred to palms, dipterocarps, Moraceae, Fagaceae and Leguminosae, while from India are recorded in the Eocene the gymnosperms, *Podocarpus* and *Araucaria*, as well as palms, bananas and so on, but in general the Tertiary fossil record is still vague.

By the early Miocene (25 m years ago), the continents looked very much as they do today, with India north of the equator and Australia only 6° south of its present position, but the Panamanian isthmus did not exist until 4 m years ago, so that only then could there be a complete mingling of the faunas of north and south America. The equids, mastodons, tapirs and llamas moved south and the sloths and armadilloes moved north, while the juxtaposition of Africa and Eurasia allowed the African elephants, bovids and pigs to migrate into Europe. Throughout this period, northern India and the Malesian archipelago were undergoing a great deal of vulcanism and mountain building, the Himalaya rising at this time, while Australasia (but not Papuasia) was stable. Australasia–

Papuasia, plus the eastern part of present-day Malesia, had separated from Antarctica about 53 m years ago, two million or so years after India had collided with Laurasia. Earlier, a portion of Australasia may have split off and become embedded in what is now present-day south Tibet and Burma–Thailand, or may have gone down the trench south of Java (4). By the latter half of the Tertiary, South America and Africa were free of major flooding, as were India and Australia but, at its highest levels, the sea covered half of present-day Sumatra and Java, the Philippines, Sulawesi and all but the highest parts of New Guinea. The Gulf of Carpentaria in northern Australia and much of the east side of continental Asia may well have been dry land.

The Quaternary is remarkable for its climatic fluctuations, with advancing and retreating icecaps and glaciers. These fluctuations were already beginning to build up in the Pliocene about 3.2 m years ago, and it appears that there have been 17 glacial advances and their interglacials in the last 1.7 m years. Although there is some relation between glacial advance and the enlarging of deserts, there is still much work to be done in this connection, as there is in the interpretation of palynological evidence on the depression of vegetation belts. Part of this derives from the breadth of ecological tolerance of some species known today. For example, in a model study, Hall and Swaine (5) have shown that the living *Sloetiopsis usambarensis* (Moraceae) occupies dry coastal forest in Ghana but, in Ivory Coast, this plant is found in much wetter, even evergreen, forest. Again, one of the typical lowland evergreen forest trees of Ghana is *Angylocalyx oligophyllus* (Leguminosae) but in Nigeria this tree is widespread in dry semi-deciduous forest. Dangers can be deduced even from temperate floras wherever ecologically different but closely allied (vicariant) species occur: would their pollen grains indicate their peccadilloes? Clearly, assemblages of plants must be and are being used in reconstructions, but much remains to be done to give a completely satisfactory picture of tropical palaeoecology in the Quaternary.

During the Quaternary, the sea-level fell by up to 180 m by present-day standards, and it has been estimated that rainfall was then some 30 % less than it is now. There have certainly been fluctuations in the upper limits of forest growth but it would appear that that is exceptionally high at present and that we are witnessing an unusually high rainfall regime. In short, until relatively recently in palaeoecological time, there was a more seasonal climate. This ties in with arguments from plant distributions and the location of high levels of endemism, where refugia of rain forest organisms have been postulated in the Quaternary of Africa and South

America and it has been argued that these have since contracted and expanded.

Interglacials differ in their faunas and floras and even the last one in Britain was different from the present one: *Picea abies* was a native tree, while tropical coral reefs were more widespread, as was the giant clam, now restricted to the western Pacific. Further back, in the mid-Pleistocene of Britain, there occurred a rhinoceros closely allied to one now restricted to Indonesia, and a pig similar to one living in Borneo now: indeed, much of the European mammalian fauna was like that of the tropical Asia of today.

In summary, the reconstruction of the history of rain forest or other vegetation on any site in the tropics is an exceedingly complicated task, though recent work in a Borneo peat swamp (5) where forest deposits overlie grassland deposits again suggest a previously more seasonal climate locally. Nevertheless, certain patterns of animal and plant distribution raise fascinating questions, some of which have been resolved through the work of geologists and palaeoecologists. Possibly the most celebrated is Wallace's Line (4) which divides the Asiatic and Australasian faunas in the eastern part of Indonesia. The marsupials are to the east of the line and have an origin somewhere in Gondwanaland, the placentals largely to the west. There are similar distinctions in other animal groups but it is less clear-cut in plants. The geological history of Malesia shows that both plants and animals could have reached the area, without crossing water, from Laurasia, and from Gondwanaland *via* either Australia or India. The explanation of the enigmatic nature of Sulawesi, which puzzled Wallace, is thought to be that it has part of its origin in Australasia–Papuasia and part in the Asiatic block. Either side of it are the two great rain-forest areas of Malesia, Sumatra–Malaya–Borneo and New Guinea, in which there is no general sign in their geological history of the desiccations found in that of Africa and South America. In New Guinea are represented many of the Austral elements typical of Australasia but, in West Malesia, these are found chiefly in the heath-forest flora. In Malesia two previously isolated faunas and floras mingle and in the angiosperms are the overlapping north-south plant group affinities elsewhere more separated: Ericaceae/Epacridaceae, Magnoliaceae/Winteraceae, Saxifragaceae/Escalloniaceae, to name a selection (4). Biogeographers may therefore be tempted to argue (and it would be very convenient) that the piece of Australia now in Burma or melted under Java held the 'cradle of the angiosperms'.

2.2   Tropical climate

The equatorial position of tropical rain forest ensures that more radiation strikes it than strikes forests outside the tropics and that there is no winter period associated with reduced daylength. Nevertheless, the tropics do not comprise a region of uniform climate, owing to the position of the continental masses, air-flow and sea-currents leading to wide variations in precipitation, relative humidity, temperature, wind and vulnerability to violent storms and so on. This pattern of macroclimate largely governs the general pattern of forest type distribution. As an example, the present-day rain forest of West Africa is split in two by the Dahomey Gap or Interval. Here the coastline runs WSW–ENE, the prevalent winds make an acute angle with the coast, and little moisture is brought ashore. To the north and south of the forest area, the dry Saharan and somewhat wetter South African anti-cyclonic systems support a rain forest–savanna mosaic, open woodland, dry savanna and grasslands (6).

2.2.1   *Precipitation*

Tropical climates have been divided into five major categories: rainy tropical, monsoon tropical, wet-and-dry tropical, tropical semi-arid and tropical arid. These are not, of course, sharply separable in the field but rain forest in this book is found only under the régimes of the first two. The others support savanna vegetation, or drier formations, like deserts. The major areas with a rainy tropical climate, i.e. the Amazon basin, parts of Central America, the Congo basin, the steep eastern slopes of Madagascar and much of Malesia, have more than 2000 or even 3000 mm of precipitation per annum, more or less evenly distributed throughout the year, and bear tropical rain forest. However, the semi-deciduous forests of Burma, for example, may not have a different overall precipitation but it is markedly seasonal. Precipitation in rain forest may reach 10 000 mm, which has been recorded in West Africa, but there is always some seasonal fluctuation. Increasing fluctuations are associated with different vegetation types like the African savannas which have a lower standing crop and are believed to be less productive (6). Conversely, the very wettest regions may also be less productive, which has been explained as being due to poorer growth associated with high levels of leaching, as in the Rio Negro region of Brazil, while greater cloudiness has also been suggested as limiting growth rates (6).

The major source of moisture is rainfall, of which 25 % may be lost through canopy evaporation. Some 40 % may trickle down limbs and trunks and be partly absorbed by bark and epiphytes and partly evaporated within the forest, so that it has been estimated that in Malaysia only some 10% of the rainfall reaches the ground. In a detailed study at Pasoh, Malaysia (7), valuable distinctions were made between the effects on a 'per storm' basis, on a monthly and on an annual basis. Stem-flow was found to be 0 to 2.65 % of the precipitation on a per storm basis, from 0.32 to 0.92 % on a monthly and 0.64 % on an annual basis. Throughfall ranged from 0.0 to 99.01 % on a per storm basis, 65.27–94.64 % on a monthly basis and 77.56 % on an annual one. The interception varied from 0.15 to 100 % per storm, 5.04 to 34.31 % per month, and this represented an annual rate of 21.8 %. Other sources of moisture are dew, fog and clouds, which are of great importance in maintaining certain montane forests in tropical regions (8).

Rain gauges may therefore be very inaccurate measures of the water régime. Of the annual precipitation in a forest on the Rio Negro in Amazonia (9), some 3664 mm, about 47 %, was lost through transpiration, supporting the contention that 48 % of the precipitation in the Amazon basin is derived from the vegetation there. This compares with figures of 12 % in other non-forested parts of the world and suggests that tree-dominated landscapes are more efficient than other forms of land-use in this respect. Run-off and evaporation from the ground will be greater in forests with punctured canopies and, in large gaps, dew may form. But even intact forest may lose more water through evapotranspiration than it gains from precipitation for, in Malaysia, periods of up to a week of cloudless hot days and cold nights have been recorded, leading to just this state of affairs. Within the forest, then, there will be local variation in water availability.

There are also great variations in relative humidity. In the canopy this may fall to 70 %, whereas within the forest it is likely to remain around 90 % in the day and 95 % or above at night. Longman and Jeník (6) have argued that slow evaporation in the lower reaches of the forest may lead to a slow uptake of ions and thus to slower growth on the forest floor. They have shown that 90 % of forest undergrowth species have leaves with drawn-out 'drip-tips' and that the removal of these tips extends the drying period after rain of the blade from 20 to 90 minutes. Some trees, such as the African *Lophira alata* (Ochnaceae), have such tips when they are juvenile and in the undergrowth, but not when they reach the canopy, and Longman and Jeník have suggested that the xeromorphic features of canopy leaves may be adaptations to moisture stress. In some plants the drip-tip drainage is supplemented by other mechanisms. *Machaerium arboreum* (Leguminosae), a liane of the Panamanian forest, sheds water, or avoids the wetting of the leaves through thigmonastic and nyctinastic movements, i.e. those promoted by touch and by nightfall respectively, which are frequently found in this family (10). The drip-tips facilitate drainage, as has been verified by excision experiments, but the leaflets of the compound leaves fold together at night, when not photosynthesizing, and respond to light rain during the day by closing through the thigmonastic mechanism.

Some storms are very violent and are termed cyclones, typhoons or hurricanes. These are much rarer in the tropics than out of them (11) and they develop in specific areas at particular times of the year: in the tropical north Atlantic from June to November, in the north Pacific off Central America from June to October, in the western North Pacific from May to November (though this area is prone to strong storms throughout the year), the Bay of Bengal in May, June, October and November, the south Pacific west of 140° W from December to April and the south Indian Ocean from November to May. No such storms have been recorded from the south Atlantic or the south Pacific east of 140°W. Tropical cyclonic systems carry air-masses north (India, Mexico, Florida) or south (East Africa, Madagascar) and thus extend the tropical climate conditions beyond the geographical tropics. The importance of such cyclones which, in the western Pacific at least, are becoming more prevalent nearer the equator, will be considered in Chapter 4.

2.2.2 *Temperature and radiation*

The mean annual temperature in rain forest regions is about 27°C, ranging, on monthly average, from 24–28°C, so that seasonal variations are smaller than diurnal ones, which may be as much as 10°. Maximum temperatures rarely exceed 38°C, which is lower than in continental North America or Europe. It is unusual for the temperature to fall below 20°C, though it may reach lower levels at the base of high mountains or in the bottom of valleys. Within the forest, diurnal fluctuations vary. In Ivory Coast (6) in December the fluctuation was some 10.8° at 46 m but only 4.4° at 1 m above the ground, while in June the figures were 4.0 and 1.7° respectively. The soil temperature probably never exceeds 30°C in closed forest though may be 50°C or more in the surface layers of exposed soil. At a depth of 75 cm no discernible diurnal fluctuations were measurable in closed forest.

The effective daylength for emergent trees on the equator is $12\frac{3}{4}$ hours, though less inside the forest or on steep slopes. At 5° north or south, the annual variation in daylength is half an hour; at 10° it is one hour and at 17° it is two. The light that reaches the forest floor is of three types. There are shafts of light passing between leaves, sunflecks, which appear to move as the earth moves with respect to the sun; light through perforations in the canopy; and light reflected from leaf and branch surfaces, with that transmitted through one or more leaves. It has been calculated that the total radiation reaching the forest floor is some 2–3 % of the incident light energy. In Malaysia, it has been estimated that half of the annual total is from flecks, 6 % from canopy holes and 44 % reflected or transmitted. In gaps, this last is a much smaller component than in closed forest and the proportion of far-red light and infra-red is thus lower, for in closed forest these are the wavelengths transmitted through photosynthesizing tissue. This change may be registered in a plant through its phytochrome system, indicating that its leaves are no longer in shade.

Many herbs in the ground vegetation of rain forest have brightly-coloured leaves, which make them colourful foliage plants for the dingy houses of man. These colours are seen in *Begonia*, for example, and are due to anthocyanins which were traditionally held to enhance transpiration by increasing heat absorption (12). When four angiosperms with such colours were tested in Malaysia, however, no temperature differences could be discerned. In each of them the anthocyanin was confined to a single layer just below the photosynthetic tissue, and it now seems that the layer back-scatters light for photosynthesis.

CHAPTER THREE

SOILS AND NUTRIENTS

3.1 Tropical soils

Tropical soils are rather more diverse than is widely believed, for the well-known, highly-weathered and leached soils cover only half of the tropical land surface (1), but these 'latosols' are a common feature of rain-forest country. Pedologists classify soil types according to various systems and give the different layers recognizable in profiles different names. The system set out by Burnham (2) is perhaps most comprehensible and is the basis of what follows.

The upper layers or horizons, from the surface towards the underlying geological material, are litter, sometimes partly decayed plant material and well-decomposed humus. When the last does not pass imperceptibly into the layers below, it is known as *mor*, a humus type that develops in aerobic conditions, while, in anaerobic conditions, a peat may form. A *mull* soil is where the surface layer is incorporated with mineral particles and underlies a thin litter layer. Layers with well-integrated humus and minerals are known as A horizons, beneath which lie the weathered layers or B horizons. These are subdivided or may be separated from the A horizon by layers of deposition of iron or aluminium compounds. The C horizon is the parent material.

3.1.1 *Soil processes*

With warmth and copious rainfall, the humid tropics have strong weathering of the soil so that minerals are continuously leached from the upper

24

layers. The moisture and warmth in a tropical soil promote rapid breakdown of vegetable and other organic matter by decomposers. The weathering allows the development of deep soils which may reach 15 m or more in profile, though very often this is deeper than the levels to which the decomposing material reaches, so that the biologically significant layers lie over considerable depths of saprolite, or 'rotten rock'.

The weathering of all the common minerals, except quartz, to clay and oxides of iron and aluminium leads to the formation of soils which are more clayey than in temperate regions. Furthermore, the great depth of the parent material means that erosion rarely removes or even reaches the unweathered nutrient-rich parent soils. Therefore not only the superficial soils are low in nutrients: eroded slopes and transported materials such as alluvium are also. Leaching means that sodium, potassium, calcium and magnesium are often at very low concentrations in tropical soils, though acidity is also low. The clay of most well-developed, well-drained tropical soils does not swell and shrink on wetting and drying, so that the cracking familiar in temperate-zone clays is rare. This kaolinitic clay has a low cation-exchange capacity, so that its nutrient-holding capacity is mainly a function of humus content and is low where that is low. This is true of subsoils, so that roots tend to be concentrated in the surface soil and few are below, even though it may be physically not difficult to penetrate. The rapid rate of decomposition in well-drained soils leads to a thin litter layer and low levels of organic matter in the soil, although termites may be of local importance in transporting rotting wood to great depths in their galleries and chambers.

3.2 Soil types

While considerable edaphic variation occurs within a small area such as the Malay Peninsula, the average properties in terms of exchangeable cation content, and thus fertility, are commonly found, extreme soil types being rare, so that there appears to be great uniformity. However, the soils can be rather varied in colour and texture and are now grouped into three major categories.

3.2.1 Major groups of soils

Ultisols (red-yellow podzols) are distinguished by their B horizon which has 20 % or more clay than in adjacent horizons, the fine clay particles being considered to have been brought in from the upper layers in suspension. This layer may be bright yellow-brown or reddish, but the distinct pale horizon associated with podzols in temperate regions is usually absent. These soils are low in bases, and despite their high contents of weatherable materials, leaching makes them infertile. They are commoner under seasonal climates than they are in the wetter regions of the Malesian region, though in Africa they are found on the Upper and Middle Pleistocene erosion surfaces.

On the more extensive older surfaces in Africa there are *oxisols*. These are rare in the Malesian region, probably largely due to extensive recent orogeny. They have an oxic horizon in the subsoil and are often coloured dark red. Their clay content is high but they are less sticky than ultisols and roots may penetrate easily. In Malesia they are leached, but are marginally more fertile than ultisols nearby unless they occur on siliceous materials like alluvium, when they may have high levels of quartz sand and may be less fertile. *Alfisols* are rather like ultisols but have a higher base concentration and hence greater fertility.

These main groupings intergrade and many soils are completely inter-mediate: indeed, as there is no readily discernible correlation with fertility levels it has been argued that there is a good case for abandoning such names.

The term 'laterite' is used where there has been redistribution and concentration of sesquioxides in the soil profile. It is most common in seasonal climates or areas drier than the tropics bearing rain forest. Often there is a layer in the subsoil with compact clay mottled bright red and pale yellow or grey. Such clay impedes root penetration and in hardened laterites prevents it, so that these soils are seen to be rather infertile though they are not necessarily more weathered than comparable non-lateritic soils.

3.2.2   *Volcanic soils*

Where there is volcanic activity as, for example, in Java, there is a new input of fresh mineral material. Magmas low in silica appear as lava, those higher, in the form of ash, which is fragments of pumice. Newly-formed soils over lava resemble brown earths and, in time, become oxisols. The weathering of ash, on the other hand, leads to the formation of *andosols*, which contain allophane, an association of hydrous silica and alumina with a large active surface. This last feature gives the soil a high porosity and a low bulk density, with a 'fluffy' consistency, a high water retention capacity, high levels of cation exchange and a capacity to form stable associations of mineral and fine organic matter which give the upper layers a characteristic dark colour. In humid regions, allophane eventually turns into kaolinite in a matter of thousands of years so that andosols occur only in late Pleistocene and Quaternary ash. In a world context, they are moderately fertile, but in the humid tropics they are the most fertile of all, though phosphorus and some minor elements such as manganese may be deficient. Once dried out, though, andosols may be irredeemable, for a hard pan of cemented silica or of iron and other oxides may form at a depth of 40–100 cm and this is not readily penetrated by roots. Nevertheless, it is on such soils as these that the intensive agriculture of Java with its high concentration of people is based. Furthermore, the ash from volcanoes may spread very far, enriching soils which are not typical andosols.

3.2.3   *Other soil types*

Of other soil types represented in the tropics, mention should be made of the *podzols* which resemble those in northern Europe. They lie over predominantly quartz parent material, low in clay and bases, and have a bleached horizon below the humic layer and a dark or brightly coloured B horizon rich in colloidal organic material, sometimes with sesquioxides. Such soils are commonly found in old beach deposits which are now inland, but also occur on sandstone, quartzite or acidic volcanic deposits, and are covered with heath forest. They have very low fertility and a low capacity to retain water or cations. Soils over limestone formations, including the jagged karst landscapes (Fig. 3) peculiar to the tropics, may be brownish-red latosols or, in heavy rainfall areas, highly humic soils. Over ultrabasic rocks with high levels of iron and manganese, low levels of silica and high concentrations of such toxic elements as nickel, chromium and cobalt, the soils resemble the oxisols on basic igneous rocks, but they are as variable as the forests they bear. Of alluvial soils, those marine ones colonized by mangroves are, of course, saline and are alkaline to neutral. With consolidation, acidity rises and there is an increase in organic material. Soil micro-organisms reduce sulphate ions, which react with iron to give pyrite and ferrous sulphide. As rain- and fresh water replaces the saline, the mangrove becomes peat-swamp forest or, later, freshwater swamp forest with soils which are generally very fertile and have been much exploited for agriculture. Alluvial soils deposited in lakes or by rivers are of varying fertility dependent on the age of the eroding materials and whether they are overlain with peat, in which case fertility may be rather good. In mountainous regions, rainfall greatly

Figure 3   Forest and chasmophytes on the rugged karst limestone of the Malay Peninsula. The palm at the bottom left. *Maxburretia rupicola*, is restricted to these limestones.

affects the forest soil type. On seasonally dry mountains, organic matter content increases with altitude, and shallower soils occur because there is less weathering. On wetter mountains, there are peaty soils, which support 'cloud forest'. These soils are leached, podzolized or waterlogged, with a reduction in microbiological activity, and are thus of low fertility.

3.3   The relationship between soils and forest type

Already it has been pointed out that andosols will support intensive agriculture and that podzols support only heath forest. Can other correlations be found? Under increasingly well-watered, but not swampy, conditions, the density of emergent trees increases and there is a higher incidence of crown epiphytes and of lianes. On fertile sites under such conditions there is a significant increase in the percentage of deciduous species. With decreased nutrient availability and sharply drained soils, there is a decline in stature and density of emergents. In areas of impeded drainage, such as some alluvial regions, the majority of rain forest trees may not thrive so that there are fewer constituent species and even single-dominant stands, notably of palms, such as the *Metroxylon* swamps of New Guinea and the *Nypa* stands in Malesian mangrove forests. Peat-swamp forests are well known in Sumatra, Malaya and Borneo, very rare in Africa but better represented in the Amazon, some islands in the Caribbean and the north coast of the Guyanas, and have a rather restricted flora. The peat usually has a pH of less than 4.0 and may be up to 20 m deep with a solid layer over depths of semiliquid material with rotting wood. No bird or mammal is known to be restricted in its distribution to such forests. Freshwater swamp forest differs in being regularly inundated with mineral-rich fresh water with a pH greater than 6.0 and in having a shallow peat layer. It is associated with the great tropical rivers of many parts of the world, as in Indochina, large parts of Africa, and South America, notably along the Amazon and the Rio Negro. There, the floodplains spread widely and the distinction between the seasonally flooded (*várzea*), the permanently inundated (*igapó*) and that which is never inundated (*terra firme*) is of great importance for settlement and agriculture. Such forests are not distinct in terms of the families of plants involved but there is, as in the example of *Metroxylon*, a tendency to greater gregariousness. This is important from a commercial point of view in the Borneo swamp forests, as ramin (*Gonystylus bancanus*) grows there in rather pure stands, making its exploitation worthwhile. Mangrove swamps are poor in species and consist of largely facultative halophytes.

The fauna, as far as, for example, the birds of West Malaysia are concerned, is rather distinctive and comprises largely the species typical of cleared land and gardens, to which such birds may have spread. Of uninundated forest types, the heath forest is found on the poor siliceous soils of the Malay Peninsula, Indochina, Borneo, and in New Guinea, where it is mostly scattered. It occurs in the Amazon basin, the Rio Negro being black through draining it, and in a small coastal sand area in Gabon. It consists of saplings and poles, all rather tidy and orderly but low, dense and impenetrable with no trace of layering. In Borneo, this is the *kerengas* forest rich in the secondary-consumer plants, the insectivorous pitcher plants, *Nepenthes*, and sundews, *Drosera*. In the Amazon, it is the *caatinga*, which is also found in the Guyanas. It occurs in disjunct pockets but on the Rio Negro covers hundreds to thousands of square kilometres. The trees are markedly sclerophyllous, like the trees of cloud forest mentioned below; on nearby soils with only as much as 5% clay there is distinctly different non-sclerophyllous forest. In the *caatinga*, the trees commonly coppice and the roots may make up 60% of the biomass, whereas on oxisols this figure is nearer 20% (3). The roots form mats in the slowly decomposing litter and may be picked up like a carpet. Such forests have a low resistance to fire. In the Malesian forests, the fauna is largely of animals found in other forest types though some groups, like snakes in Borneo, may be poorly represented.

Forests on ultrabasics are often low and may consist of shrubby vegetation juxtaposed to high rain forest, as in parts of Sulawesi and New Caledonia. In the Solomon Islands, geologists have been able to map the rocks from aerial photographs of the forests, though such vegetation on ultrabasics in West Malesia is less distinctive. Forests on limestone are found in parts of the Caribbean and Malesia but are absent from the African humid tropics. They have a large number of plant species restricted to them and the caves formed in them have been used by man for a very long time. In the moistest regions, limestone may carry seasonal forests, while on fertile alluvium and basalts in seasonal regions, there may be 'moist' forests.

The wet montane forests on peaty soils have scleromorphic leaves despite the cloud cover; indeed, cut shoots of trees from such forests in Jamaica and Malaya (4) show resistance to water stress no superior to lowland rain-forest trees, and are far less efficient at stopping water loss than are the sclerophyllous plants of, for example, the Mediterranean. It has been suggested that the scleromorphic features here, and indeed in lowland forest, therefore have nothing to do with water stress, but are possibly associated with the edaphic conditions, though they remain enigmatic.

Are the differences in soils under typical lowland rain forest also reflected in the species composition of the forest? In northwest Colombia (5), chemical comparisons were made between the leaves, epiphyllae, epiphytes, litter and soil at six sites. There were significant differences in soil composition, but in the vegetable material, only potassium and caesium levels differed. There was a loose correspondence between soils and geological substrate but apparently little between soils and the vegetation.

It has been argued that forest development is much quicker than soil development, so that vegetation mapping can scarcely be predictive of soil type (6). Nevertheless, in the rain forests of Australia there seem to be good correlations between distribution of forest types and nutrient concentrations, particularly phosphorus, nitrogen, potassium and calcium (1), and soil fertility overrides latitudinal climatic factors. In Brazil, a strong correlation has been reported between height, density and other parameters of forest structure, and soil features. At a microhabitat level, the effect of trees (stationary, long-lived organisms) on local depletion of nutrients may be marked. Around dipterocarp roots there may be bleached sands, while allelopathic exudates, including phenolics leached from leaves, may also affect the local soil conditions.

3.4 Nutrient cycling

Because of the lack of absolute synchrony of soil and forest development it has been argued (6) that tropical rain forest often becomes independent of soil, efficiently recycling its nutrients. It has been calculated (2) that the rapid release of nutrients in decomposition is matched by rapid re-utilization and that the annual return of nutrients to the soil is some three to four times that in temperate forests. In the Central Amazon basin (7), the soils and parent material have been greatly weathered so that the present-day soils are clays, low in nutrients, consisting of kaolinite with sands from the ancient Brazilian and Guiana Shields. Jordan (7) has shown that the leaching of nutrients from the soil in the forests there was less than or equal to the input from the atmosphere every year between 1975 and 1980 and concluded that the weathering of the parent material does not contribute in a major way to the nutrient economy of the system. In short, the forest apparently maintains itself on the nutrients derived from the atmosphere. Attention is thus focused on the nutrient-conserving mechanisms in cycling.

In the Amazonian forest of southern Venezuela, Jordan and his colleagues (8) found that the nutrients reaching the ground in gaps were more concentrated than in closed forest and suggested that they were absorbed by epiphytic algae and lichens and possibly leaf-surfaces. Bromeliads, living as epiphytes in the canopy, can absorb canopy leachate through the reservoir at the heart of the plant (9). It has also been shown in Puerto Rico that epiphyllae (small plants growing on leaves) enhance cation absorption from precipitation some 1.7 to 20 times (10). A new explanation for the presence of drip-tips in rain forest (11) argues that soil structure may be less affected and leaching retarded where the incident raindrop size is small and that the tips act as spouts promoting just this. This might get round the problem of why drip-tips are not found in all ever-wet communities if leaf drainage amelioration is the only function of the tips.

The fall of leaves, bracts, flowers, fruits, twigs, branches and whole trees constitutes the major input of nutrients to the upper layers of the rain forest soils but the measure of this input is difficult, great variations being found at particular sites, and no particular generalizations about the relationship between litter fall and soil nutrient status can be made.

Litter in *Araucaria hunsteinii* forest in New Guinea represents some 5 % of the biomass and is formed at a rate of some 8.7 t per ha per year (12). Although the living leaves represent only 5 % of the living biomass, they hold some 23.5 % of its nutrients. Under different canopies in Puerto Rico, different rates of decomposition were found, the fastest being under *Euterpe globosa*, while amongst the six common species tested, there was great variation in the rate of decomposition as well (13). The rates are such that whole trees may completely disappear in ten years or less, a factor which must be remembered in plot reassessments (14).

Leaf- and other litter falling into streams might appear to be a potentially important drain on the system in terms of nutrient losses, but recent work in Hong Kong (15) suggests that breakdown in streams is extremely rapid; macro-invertebrate populations show spatial and temporal segregation which increases cycling efficiency, so that tropical stream systems may in fact act as nutrient conservation enhancers.

3.4.1   *Roots and mycorrhizae*

Within the forest itself, the most important mechanisms involved in nutrient cycling are the roots. In the Amazon basin, Jordan and Herrera (16) have found that the poorer the soils, the shallower the mat of roots and surface humus, and that, in the poorest, the mat may be only 15–40 cm deep, with 58 % of the feeding roots within it. Direct physical adsorption of labelled cations sprinkled on root mats was 99.9 %, and when the tracers were added in the form of labelled leaves, no detectable radioactivity leached through.

Work *in vitro* has shown that mycorrhizae are important here. Most plant species are capable of forming root associations with the Endogonaceae, a family of Zygomycetes, to form what are known as vesicular-arbuscular mycorrhizae. There is, apparently, a complete lack of specificity of the host. It is possible that such mycorrhizae improve water uptake as well. Ectotrophic mycorrhizae are found in only three species besides pines (17), the dipterocarps, and also in the caesalpinioid group of Leguminosae. Over 60 % of these do not form nodules with nitrogen-fixing bacteria, and those with the mycorrhiza have no root hairs (18). There is some evidence to suggest that the fungi are antagonistic to certain other, pathogenic, fungi and it is well known that pines do not develop beyond the nursery stage without their mycorrhiza. Furthermore, some legumes do not nodulate on phosphorus-deficient soil unless their mycorrhiza is there. On very poor soils, species with obligate mycorrhizal associations are likely to predominate and root-hairs become redundant, because these latter overlap too much and compete, whereas mycorrhizal hyphae are better dispersed. Indeed, many obligate mycotrophs, particularly in rain forest, have no root-hairs. Vesicular-arbuscular mycorrhizae extract minerals from the soil solution while some ectomycorrhizae may break down the litter, directly recycling nutrients, but these mycorrhizae are more demanding of their hosts too. Nutrient recovery is increased when roots form the dense mats typical of the poorest soils (19).

In the root mat, there may be other nutrient-conserving mechanisms. Algae might take up dissolved nutrients to be released on their de-composition, while there are nitrogen-fixing micro-organisms, both nodular and free-living. Furthermore, it must not be forgotten that a good deal of litter is not at ground level but is deposited in the crotches of trees, in the masses of epiphytes or the crowns of certain dwarf treelets in the lower reaches of the forest. Such sparsely-branched treelets as species of *Semecarpus* (Anacardiaceae) of Malesia have buds and leafbases sur-rounded by rotting humus.

The role of termites in redistributing organic material is very important. In Zaïre, some 870 termite colonies per ha were found in rain forest. This represents 16 t of biomass which immobilizes some 2.6 t per ha of organic matter, 0.7 t of calcium and 61 kg of nitrogen, while some 6 t of plant matter may have been consumed. At Pasoh, West Malaysia, it is estimated that 38.8 kg of leaf litter is thus disposed of every week, which represents some 32% of the leaf fall. The role of certain other animals will be discussed in Chapter 7.

3.4.2   Leaves and leaf-fall

Another explanation for the scleromorphic leaves of trees in nutrient-poor sites argues that the relatively thick cuticle and wax deposits and relatively low water content make them resistant to nutrient loss by parasites and herbivores (16). There is some evidence that insect attack is less severe. Furthermore, the nutrients invested in leaves are used in photosynthesis for prolonged periods, are more resistant to leaching by rainfall, and a large proportion of leaf nutrients are known to be translocated out of them before abscission. In Malaysia (20) on the other hand, it has been found that the nutrients in precipitation increase through canopy leaching, which was richest in potassium, representing some 24.57 kg K per ha per year— 98% of these nutrients reached ground by throughfall and only 2% by stem-flow. Little leaching was recorded from seedlings in Puerto Rico (9) though there were measurable amounts leached from crops such as banana and sugarcane. Once more, an explanation for drip-tips can be provided: their rapid removal of water from the lamina surface may reduce the time in which leaching out of minerals takes place.

3.4.3   Overall production

The leaf-fall in the Manaus area of Brazil has been estimated at some 7 t per ha per year in a standing crop of some 900 t including roots, about 585 t dry matter. Figures from other parts of the world are: 289 for Ghana, 469 for Ivory Coast, 664 for Malaya and 400 in *terra firme* forest in the Amazon (21). More than three-quarters of the carbon in the system is in the wood, whereas in temperate coniferous woodland, half of it is in the soil.

   In tropical forests, except where peat is accumulating, the net production of mature forest is nil. The largest trees may in fact be stagnant and the earlier stages of fast-growing trees at maximum annual net production, but it is exceedingly difficult to assess net production because of the problems of sampling and the role of animals. Nevertheless, it has been estimated that the net production may be the same as that of European forests though the gross production may be twice this. The balance is due to greater losses in respiration, the forests of Europe being leafless for over half the year. The observed greater production of plantations at altitude in tropical regions has been explained as a result of depressed respiration during the cool nights but there are other differences such as soils and aspect which may have an effect too.

CHAPTER FOUR

THE CHANGING BIOLOGICAL FRAMEWORK

As von Humboldt noticed on the mountains of tropical South America, tropical forests at increasing altitudes look increasingly more like temperate ones. In the lowlands, the forest may be some 25–45 m tall, with 'emergent' trees protruding above the general canopy, whereas in lower montane forest the canopy may be at 15–33 m with fewer conspicuous emergents, and in upper montane to subalpine forests the canopy may drop to 1.5 m and there are no emergents. The 'tropical' features of cauliflory, buttresses, lianes and the common occurrence of pinnate leaves decline in frequency with altitude as they do with latitude. This may reflect to a certain extent the taxonomic groups of plants which grow at different altitudes, but such trends can be seen even within families. Conversely, the frequency of microphylls and, especially noticeably, of non-vascular epiphytes, increases with altitude, most remarkably in the bryophyte-festooned cloud forests of tropical regions.

Compared with temperate forests, however, there is a marked lack of readily recognizable strata in the lowland forests. In temperate countries, the tree-, shrub-, herb- and ground-layers are familiar in woods, but these are often a reflection of management techniques: stands may be more or less even-aged, or silvicultural practice may have removed smaller trees and bushes which might otherwise blur the clear stratification. In certain tropical forests, a stratification is clear, as in single-dominant ones such as the *Gilbertiodendron dewevrei* (Leguminosae) forests of Africa, but, in general, the most useful division that can be made in mixed tropical rain forest is between the canopy and the shaded area beneath. This can be

36

Figure 4 A forest profile some 60 m long and 8 m wide in Andalau Forest Reserve, Brunei, Borneo. Only trees over *c*. 5 m tall figured. Reproduced with permission from P. S. Ashton in *Oxford Forestry Memoirs* **25** (1964), fig. 25.

imagined as the undulating surface connecting the bases of the crowns of the large trees. Clearly this surface is constantly changing as trees grow up and eventually collapse, and the structure of the forest can only be understood in terms of these dynamics. The framework of trees between and on which other plants, fungi, bacteria and animals live and die is a result of the careers of individual trees.

4.1   Tropical rain forest successions

4.1.1   *Problems with older views*

In older textbooks, a good deal is made of the progress of succession: an orderly replacement of plant and animal species culminating in an optimal climax vegetation and associated faunal assemblages for the physical parameters of any particular region. In turn, this has led to schemes of prediction of vegetation types from the combined observations of physical parameters such as latitude, precipitation and temperature regimes.

When the nature of the successional process is scrutinized critically, however, as it has been in a classic review by Drury and Nisbet (1), it is seen that much of the accepted dogma on the nature of succession is far too rigid in its approach. Temporal sequences on one site under stable climatic regimes are the essence of secondary successions, whereas those on such sites with changing climatic conditions are primary successions, such as the changes in vegetation as a glacier retreats. Observations on what is essentially a temporal phenomenon have often been made spatially, that is, adjacent sites are seen as representative of consecutive time-stages. The observational basis of much of the older work is therefore called into question. Also attacked is the supposed orderly replacement of apparently altruistic species by their successors, for there are many examples of plants in temperate regions emitting allelopathic substances that hinder their replacement by others. Of tropical examples, some species of *Croton* (Euphorbiaceae) and *Piper* produce chemicals which inhibit seed germination, and it is thought that the Brazil nut, *Bertholletia excelsa* (Lecythidaceae), may produce toxic litter. Monospecific stands of *Dinizia excelsa* (Leguminosae) in Brazil produce a very acid humus within ten years and this supports a very specialized set of understorey plants. As has already been noted in Chapter 3, there is no requirement for a mature soil profile to herald the arrival of a 'climax' forest, so the correlation between these, again often repeated, is not universal. In short, one or more of the features classically associated with succession may not obtain in any particular vegetational change under study. Succession is seen as the sequential expression of conspicuousness reflecting the maturity rates of individuals of particular species, for so-called 'climax' species may occur, as small plants, in the early stages of such sequences.

4.1.2   *The modern interpretation*

In tropical rain forest, change is due to the refilling of gaps in the vegetation, made by the collapse of canopy trees. This process is familiar to European foresters, some of whom refer to the regenerating patches as *chablis*, a term taken up in this context by Oldeman (2). In the Old World tropics, Whitmore, taking his inspiration from the work of E. W. Jones and of A. S. Watt in European vegetation, and the African studies of

Aubréville and Hartshorn, among others, in the New, have independently come to similar conclusions on the importance of gaps in rain-forest structure. These forests, then, are seen as patchworks of regenerating gaps and new tree-falls: the essence of this structure is to be found in the understanding of how and where gaps form, by what they are filled and the biological characteristics of the fillers, both plants and animals. This approach has application in many other vegetation types, too.

The concept of the 'climax' forest as that mosaic of filling gaps, which eventually occupies any particular habitat, embraces time and therefore the unpredictable nature of the presence of any particular species at any particular point. The forest consists of patches, or islands, and potential patches, so that much of island biogeography on a small scale may be applicable to rain forest biology (3). Thus those species that thrive in newly-formed gaps may either immigrate afresh, as to islands in an otherwise disagreeably oversubscribed sea, or possibly may lurk in the seedbank ready for the 'island' when it arrives through the collapse of the vegetation above it. Again, those species which require shade when young and are referred to as shade-bearers, persist in a similar way, though as seedlings or saplings, which, quietly ticking over on the forest floor with little net growth, are as 'dormant' as seeds.

Thus forest cycling may be considered as overlapping processes of secondary succession as contrasted with primary succession, that is, the formation of vegetation on previously unvegetated sites, such as vulcano-seres on lava, while the revegetation of landslips may be considered as a rather intermediate state of affairs in that frequently some soil is left *in situ* and often plants creep in vegetatively from adjacent vegetated sites. Clearly, there may be little to choose between this and a 'large' gap formed by fire, anthropogenic or otherwise, and thence gaps formed by storms and smaller gaps made by the falling of a limb from a canopy tree. Nevertheless, it is often useful to refer to primary succession when isolated naked deposits, such as that represented by Krakatoa after its eruption in 1883, are considered. Primary succession is discussed more fully in section 4.7.

4.2   The ecology of gaps

Even during still nights in tropical rain forest, trees can be heard crashing down at alarmingly frequent intervals. Trees are not immortal and, with age, they become prone to attack by fungi, other pathogens and inverte-brates, growing 'stag-headed' and dropping branches or major limbs. There is an increase in falls in the wettest seasons, probably because the anchorage may become more precarious as run-off erodes the soil around the roots. Gusts before storms are apt to increase the likelihood of collapse but, in still weather, trees fall too and it has been suggested, on the camel's back principle, that epiphytic loads may be important in the collapse of major limbs, if not of whole trees. The fall may lead to damage to neighbouring trees, or if they are linked together by lianes, to the fall of such trees as well. Sometimes, a falling tree may be half-felled and hang, trussed up by these lianes, continuing in a small way to produce new leaves, flowers and fruits.

On the other hand, localized squalls can fell relatively huge areas: over 80 ha of *Shorea albida* forest was thus devastated at one time in Sarawak, Borneo. Some regions are more prone to such storms than are others and storm frequency is known to be increasing in some areas. To take Sarawak again, the mean number of gaps and the mean gap size increased steadily between 1947 and 1961. Lightning is an important gap-maker in the peat-swamp forests of West Malaysia and Sarawak, for fires in the accumulated dry epiphytic detritus may thus be initiated. Such fires are also well known in mangrove forests in both West Malaysia and New Guinea. Gaps thus formed differ from others in that the shade-bearing saplings are often killed as well, so that herbs initiate succession. Gaps are also formed by landslips, notably on steep river banks, where they may be constantly renewed and any succession established may be restarted each time (Fig. 5). In New Guinea and elsewhere, earthquakes are important in gap formation.

Animals may be involved in making or maintaining gaps as at salt-licks or in the perpetuation of grassy glades as by rhinoceros and other herbivores in African montane forests. More sensational have been the results of caterpillar attacks: in 1948 a 31 km strip of peat-swamp forest in Sarawak lost all its *Shorea* trees. From the observation that nests of the termite *Microcerotermes dubius* are invariably associated with patches of dead and dying trees in West Malaysia, and the fact that all such trees in gaps up to 16 × 8 m were infected by termites, it has been cogently argued that these animals, too, are important gap-makers. Possibly a gap is abandoned and the termites move on when exposure increases (4). On a smaller scale, single trees may be killed by the bark-stripping of apes, for instance orang-utans in Sumatra (5).

Gaps, then, may vary from small punctures in the canopy, caused by the loss of a limb, to huge areas of devastation. In a classic study Poore (6), working on a West Malaysian plot of some 12.24 ha with apparently stable areas of canopy some 45–50 m tall, found that it included some 10 % by

Figure 5 Landslips caused by river erosion undergoing colonization in eastern Panama. The early stage shows toppled saplings, bare ground and seedlings while the later is dominated by tree ferns. Note the unbranched pachycaul *Gustavia* sp. (Lecythidaceae), bottom left.

area of gaps with 75 fallen trees, 90 dead but not decayed trunks and 40–50 standing dead trees, all with a girth greater than 91 cm. The largest gap measured some 20×30 m and he calculated from the heights of the tallest trees that the mean gap size was some 400 m². The 165 trees which he estimated to have fallen in twelve years would thus form 6.6 ha of gaps, or a little over half of the entire area. Hartshorn has calculated, from gap size and frequency, that the turnover rate in forest at La Selva, Costa Rica, is 118 ± 27 years. Such rates greatly exceed those in temperate forests. The overall result is similar to that engendered by foresters' selective felling: the devastating effect of machinery and fire used by man is paralleled only by landslips or earthquakes, for then the substrate is greatly modified.

A gap caused by the fall of a tree represents a heterogeneous environment. The dying tree itself will be an almost impenetrable tangle of branches, twigs, leaves and epiphytes at one end and will present bare soil at the other. The rootplate often lies perpendicular to the ground, so that there will be around it areas shaded for part of the day, and soil of different depths and levels of disturbance from ground level to possibly some metres in the air. The bole will lie in the exposed vegetation of the forest floor and may persist for some years. The conditions at the edge of a gap are likely to be less harsh than those in the middle, and the middle of large gaps will be more exposed than the middle of smaller ones. Large gaps made by storms are likely to get larger, through windthrow of exposed trees at the margin.

In short, gaps are variable in size and frequency in both space and time: they are unpredictable.

4.3 The ecology of pioneers

4.3.1 Pioneers and shade-bearers

The variety of ecological opportunities offered by gaps is met by the differing response of different forest species to gap conditions. Species waiting for the collapse of their superiors, shade-tolerant plants generally referred to as *shade-bearers*, can be contrasted with those which are stimulated to germinate by the new conditions and known conveniently as weed trees or *pioneers*. There is a spectrum of responses to gap formation and the terms used may seem to make the process of gap colonization simpler than it really is, but as long as it is remembered that not every pioneer species necessarily has all the features associated with the pioneering 'syndrome', this should not occur.

Besides the pioneers, the trees of the successional cycles in rain forest may be conveniently divided into three groups (7): the shade-bearing trees with a light requirement for growth beyond the sapling stage; those that are similar but appear to grow merely better when a gap is formed; and those which spend their whole lives under the canopy. Examples of these can be found in rain forests all over the tropics, though it must be remembered that these categories are merely points in a spectrum. In parallel, in different families of trees, in different continents, these 'syndromes' have evolved.

At La Selva, Hartshorn (8) found that the bulk of the tree species, some 150, were shade-intolerant. A few were pioneers, the majority later successional gap-fillers. Factors affecting the presence or absence of any particular species included timing of gaps, the proximity and dispersability of seeds, the gap size, the substrate conditions and density-dependent plant-herbivore relations. The pioneers may have continuous seeding and dormancy but the gap-fillers do not, the absence of which facility may be counterbalanced by the build-up of a 'bank' of dormant saplings on the forest floor. The pioneers are generally more palatable to insects and other herbivores than are the later gap-fillers, though at La Selva there was some evidence that the common species were less palatable than rarer ones. The leaves are often large and thin, with a high turnover rate, and may be greatly perforated by herbivores: a twenty-year-old stand of *Cecropia* (Moraceae), *Dillenia*, *Musanga* (Moraceae), *Macaranga* (Euphorbiaceae) or *Cestrum* (Solanaceae) may have up to 20% of the lamina removed in this way (9). Leaves well protected by toxins, thick layers of hairs, waxes or sclerophyllous form may be present but (particularly the last) are exceptional. The gradient of palatability associated with the gap-filling in the tropics is not found in such harsher climates as saltwater swamps, semi-deserts or alpine communities where there is little change in palatability with succession.

4.3.2 Pioneer morphology

The form of many pioneers is such that they have many vertical or inclined pithy stems with their large leaves in a single layer. Sometimes the stems are inhabited by ants. The later trees have a more marked apical dominance, much layered foliage, and deep roots (often tap roots). Some have nitrogen-fixing mechanisms, as in the roots of *Albizia* (Leguminosae) or the leaves of *Anthocephalus chinensis* (Rubiaceae), and some are deciduous.

The wood of many fast-growing tropical pioneer species has thin-walled cells with large lumina and is structurally 'cheap'. With a specific gravity of 0.04 to 0.4, these include most of the world's lightest woods. Again, in harsher environments, the distinction between early and late successional plants is less obvious, so that, for example, wood of early successional legumes in drier environments has a specific gravity greater than 1.0.

The tropical pioneers grow at great speeds when young; for example *Trema micrantha* (Ulmaceae) in Costa Rica attains some 9 m in its first year and more than 30 m in eight years. Their life-span tends to be brief by comparison with later successional species. In New Guinea, the long-lived pioneers, species of *Albizia* and *Octomeles* (Datiscaceae), were found to be dying when 84 years old, whereas over-mature *Shorea curtisii* trees in West Malaysia are estimated by ^{14}C dating to have been some 800 ± 100 years old and, in Brazil, a *Bertholletia excelsa*, 14 m in girth, was estimated to be 1400 years old. Pioneers such as *Cecropia* and *Carica*, the papaya, are capable of rapid development without mycorrhizae and in this they resemble some early colonist temperate herbs which have no known mycorrhizal associations. Of micro-organisms less, in general, is known of their population changes and cycles associated with gap formation, however.

4.3.3 Features of regeneration

Periods of leaflessness in the more seasonal tropical forests may be important in the regeneration of light-demanding species of all kinds. *Cecropia*, however, will colonize only gaps at least 400 m^2 in area and it is suggested that the microclimate in smaller gaps may be inimicable to it. Balsa, *Ochroma lagopus* (Bombacaceae), seeds germinate best if they have been heated to 40°C, a temperature reached only in large gaps with little shading. In large gaps, lianes compete with shade-intolerant and pioneer tree species and only the pioneers may grow fast enough to get away. On Barro Colorado Island, Panama, it has been shown (10) that there were 1974 lianes per ha in what is semi-deciduous forest. In the same area some 22 % of the erect seedlings less than 2 m tall were liane seedlings. They are often detrimental to the hosts with which they reach the canopy, for host growth rate is decreased and mortality increased by their presence. Because the pioneer species can outstrip them, however, they cannot completely overcome regenerating forests.

Small gaps made artifically in Java refilled with primary forest trees without pioneers. Larger gaps became a tangle of such plants and went through a 'secondary' succession. There has been some debate as to whether pioneers exist in large seedbanks beneath high forest or whether the seeds are constantly added to forest, should it be in a gap phase or not. In northern Thailand (11), seeds of pioneering species of *Macaranga*, *Mallotus* (Euphorbiaceae), *Melastoma* and *Trema*, found up to 20 cm below the surface of the soil and up to 175 m from the nearest source trees, were found to be viable, though in less seasonal West Malaysia (12) few of the pioneer species examined had prolonged seed dormancy. Furthermore, pioneers are notorious for the speed with which they can colonize roadsides and abandoned cultivation. A remarkable example described by Whitmore (13) is that of a tree, *Glochidion tetrapteron* (Euphorbiaceae), known only from two gatherings until, some 50 km from the *locus classicus*, a new road was built where about 12 000 plants appeared.

Seed dormancy of such pioneers in the American tropics is apparently rare (8). Some trees there seem to have rather continuous seed production: *Cecropia obtusifolia*, for example, produces viable seed in ten months out of the twelve in Costa Rica. The majority of pioneer species there produce seed annually but some miss a year, or even up to five, between crops. They are mostly dispersed by animals and are epigeal in their germination, with photosynthetic cotyledons. Because the gaps are unpredictable, it is likely that there are only a few possible source trees within dispersal distance and this first-come, first-served principle is reflected in stands of different pioneer species in apparently similar environmental conditions. Such stands suggest that the build-up of a seedbank of diverse pioneers in moist forests is rather unimportant in general. Nevertheless, there are striking exceptions such as the 'Traveller's Palm', *Ravenala madagascariensis* (Musaceae), a pioneer of Madagascar's rain forests, with seeds which may remain dormant for many years. In Costa Rica, some pioneer species persist into the canopy and become the large trees of the forest. Similarly, the tallest tree in Africa is the kapok, *Ceiba pentandra* (Bombacaceae), which is a pioneer and also persists thus (14).

4.4. Some secondary successions

4.4.1 *Africa*

Regrowth after cultivation in Nigeria is characterized by such tree-colonists as the composite, *Vernonia conferta*, and *Trema guineensis* (Ulmaceae), with which the more slowly establishing *Musanga cecropioides* germinates, to dominate the stand from year three to fifteen or twenty, when it is followed by the shade-bearers proper. In Ghana (15), the *Musanga* stage, which also includes *Macaranga* and *Ficus* spp., is taken over at about year ten by *Funtumia* (Apocynaceae), *Albizia* and *Chlorophora* (Moraceae) from which the high forest develops. Many observations on these successions have been made, as they have been in temperate regions, on abandoned cultivation. In the Ghana example, the pioneer tree stage is prefaced by coppice regrowth of the trees left in the agricultural system and a phase of herbaceous and sub-shrubby weeds and grasses, which is followed by a thicket of the lianes, such as *Adenia* (Passifloraceae), *Entada* and *Acacia* (Leguminosae). Where large gaps are formed in Ugandan rain forests, such light-demanders as the mahoganies (Meliaceae) become conspicuous, so that it has been suggested that the mahogany-rich forests of West Africa are truly secondary.

4.4.2   Asia

At Kepong, in Malaysia (16), a plot of some 0.3 ha isolated from forest seed-bearers was colonized by 21 woody species of which *Melastoma malabathricum* (Melastomataceae) was overwhelmingly dominant. As this declined, it was replaced by the rampant fern, *Dicranopteris linearis*, preventing further establishment of woody plants. Eventually this was overcome by the canopy of the initial colonizers by year 14 and, by year 30, 51 species had established themselves.

4.4.3   America

A detailed study of regeneration after clearing in Mexican rain forests (17) took into account similar large-scale gaps in which five stages of regeneration could be recognized. The first was dominated by short-lived herbs with shrub and pioneer tree seedlings and could last for months or the succession could even remain in this state if pasturing ensued. The second stage was dominated by the shrubs which shaded out the herbs and saw the appearance of shade-tolerant species, which require lower temperatures and light levels for germination. This stage could last from 6 to 18 months and is one of rapid growth dominated by the short-lived shrubs in such genera as *Piper* and *Solanum*, reaching some 1.5 to 3 m in height. The third stage, which lasted some three to ten years, was dominated by the pioneering trees of low stature: *Trema*, *Miconia* (Melastomataceae), for example, yet also contained young examples of the taller pioneers such as *Cecropia*, *Didymopanax* and *Ochroma* (balsa), which when larger, dominated the next stage which may last from ten to forty or more years. In their shade are saplings of the trees which eventually dominate the forest and reach some 25 m. The animal-dispersed pioneer species in this study have long fruiting seasons. Examination of the digestive tracts of birds showed that, out of a sample of 167 (37 different species), individuals of some six species had seeds of both *Cecropia* and *Trema*, individuals of 19 just the former and individuals of 24 just the latter.

Janzen calculated that in a fig 'seed' shadow in Costa Rica (18) created by bats depositing 'splats' at the density of some 10 per square metre over 2500 square metres, there were 367 500 fig seeds dispersed. By contrast wind-dispersed species (in the Mexican study) normally fruited during the dry season, producing large amounts of seed, which was simultaneously dispersed on days with low relative humidities. Such species thus give rise to wide and uniform seed shadows.

4.5 Features of later succession

4.5.1 *Seeds and seedlings*

Trees of the later stages of gap-regeneration rarely exhibit delayed germination. Of the small proportion that do in West Malaysia, viable seeds of species of *Intsia* (Leguminosae) and *Barringtonia* (Lecythidaceae, *sensu lato*), for example, can be picked up at any time of the year. Generally speaking, the seeds of the later successional species are larger than those of the pioneers. Such seeds allow a build-up of rooting systems for fungal infiltration at the onset of a mycorrhizal association and can withstand the demands of the initial infection. The consequently robust seedlings may be better equipped to persist under a canopy until a gap is formed. Seeds such as those of the durians, *Durio* spp. (Bombacaceae), germinate at once and those of most of the dominant trees in West Malaysian rain forests do so within a few days of dispersal. If they do not, they rot within a few weeks (12). Many of them germinate around the parent, though they are subject to insect and other predators associated with it.

In West Malaysia, seedlings of *Shorea curtisii* are much attacked by ants which eat the cotyledons, though it can be argued that such a mass diversion (for the *Shorea* produces many seeds at any one time) may draw the predators from those seedlings which have 'got away', enhancing their survival. Some 54 % of the fruits land within 20 m of the mother in this species, and of the whole crop only some 8 % were found to be viable, all of these being dispersed less than 25 m. Those that reached the maximum distance of 80 m were found to be lighter because they had been attacked by weevils (7). Such weak dispersal is found in a species with the smallest fruits in its group of the dipterocarps known as some of the merantis, and despite the fact that fruits may be carried up to a kilometre or so in high winds before storms, perhaps it is not surprising to learn that this species often grows in 'family groups'.

In those studies where wind and animal dispersal have been compared in Nigeria and the Solomon Islands, it has been concluded that animal dispersal is the more efficient. Nevertheless, wind dispersal appears to have evolved again and again within families that exhibit both fleshy fruits or seeds, associated with animal dispersal, and dry fruits, often dehiscent and with winged seeds. Such an example is the Meliaceae with the winged seeds of the commercial mahoganies, *Swietenia* and its allies, the bat-dispersed indehiscent fruits of the *lanseh*, *Lansium domesticum*, a Malesian fruit tree, and the bird-dispersed brightly coloured seeds in dehiscent capsules typical of *Turraea* and some species of *Aglaia*. Similar ranges can be found in Apocynaceae, Bignoniaceae, Bombacaceae, Lecythidaceae, Leguminosae, Malpighiaceae, Sapindaceae, Sterculiaceae and so on. Usually the wind-dispersed examples are large trees of the canopy, but in more deciduous forests these mature nearer the forest floor.

4.5.2 Saplings

The behaviour of seedlings and saplings of the later successional species has been studied in thirty natural tree-gaps on Barro Colorado Island (19). The gaps varied from 20 to 705 m² in area and in most of them the density of individual stems and species rose sharply in the first two to three years after gap formation. In the next two to four years, the density stabilized or declined as competition within the gaps increased. After six years, individuals of the pioneer species were found in gaps of all sizes but at highest densities in large ones. The density of seedlings of those later successional species found in gaps and in the understorey of closed forest did not seem to be correlated with gap size, though they grew faster, but not as fast as the pioneers, in gaps. In large gaps the pioneer, *Trema micrantha*, tended to dominate, whereas in the smaller ones *Miconia argentea* did, allowing a measure of prediction. Of pioneers that live through the successional sequence to become canopy species, a study has been made on the same island of the palm, *Socratea durissima* (20). Individuals within each size class were so distributed that the larger they were, the further apart they were, suggesting differential mortality of the smaller size-classes, possibly due to water stress in the dry season. The result is a regular distribution in old age compared with a clumped one when young. The comparison of plots of mature or 'primary' and clearly secondary forest in East Kalimantan, Borneo (21) showed that even though 'secondary' trees were in the canopy of the 'primary' forest, no seedlings of trees were in the plots, but in the secondary forest were over 70 species of the 200 or so found in the primary. By contrast, 24 % of the sapling species and 17 % of the seedling species in the 35-year-old secondary were still 'secondary species'.

4.5.3 *Effects on nutrients*

Studies of the nutrients during successional sequences (9) have shown that immobilization of nutrients occurs rapidly. Stands ten months old contained the same quantity of nutrients as a mature field of grass; a six-year-old forest dominated by *Cecropia obtusifolia* and a fourteen-year-old one dominated by *Musanga cecropioides* had immobilized almost as much phosphorus as stands fifty years old, while the levels of litter produced in *Cecropia* stands six and fourteen years old was as great as in mature forests. This is largely due to the rapid replacement of pioneer species' leaves. The leaf-area index of six-year-old *Cecropia* forest is almost the same as that of mature forest even though the height is one-third of it. By fourteen years, microclimatic conditions are very similar too.

4.5.4 *Effects beyond the gap*

So far, the contents of the gap have been considered, but the effects of the formation of a gap can be seen in the surrounding vegetation. There is a good deal of evidence of the effect on tree growth, collected by Forest Departments in the tropics, much of it published in seemingly lifeless reports. In Sarawak, measurements of figs and breadfruit allies (Moraceae) have been made over twenty years in both 'undisturbed' and logged mixed dipterocarp forests (22). In the first two years after logging, the annual growth rates in terms of annual girth increment are often up to ten times greater than in equivalent trees in the undisturbed forest. The rates decline subsequently, though there is variation within populations, some individuals growing more rapidly over successive measurement intervals, with the rest showing little growth in either logged or unlogged forest.

4.6 Animals and succession

The influence of the cyclical processes of rain forest regeneration on animals is perhaps less understood, though work on birds on Barro

Colorado Island (23) has been recently published. The debris characteristic of the early stages of gap-filling provides a focus for decomposers and a moist habitat exploited by a diverse arthropod fauna, while a wide range of birds is known to forage primarily in such gaps. By mist-netting, it was discovered that there is a greater diversity of bird species in gaps than in closed forest but that the numbers of birds were almost the same while the gap and forest assemblages of birds were quite distinct. In well-developed forest, there are low numbers of frog and toad species while ticks and even mosquitoes are uncommon (2), but in gaps and secondary forest where the canopy, the herbaceous layer in which so many animals are living, is near the ground, they become more conspicuous.

4.6.1   *Pollination and dispersal*

With succession, the mean density of individuals of tree species declines and their pollinators consequently have to travel further and would be expected, therefore, to be larger, as they tend to be (9). Plants which are wind-pollinated dominate at first, later those visited by animals do, but the number of species visited by small bees tends not to decline, though hummingbird-pollinated tree species are rare in mature forest. In each stage, brightly-coloured flowers and bracts tend to be at the top of the canopy and are usually visited by bees, whilst those at lower levels are white, cream or pale green. Nevertheless, red bird-pollinated flowers tend to be more evenly spread vertically. This range of colour and its distribution remains rather constant as succession progresses, whereas in temperate or semi-arid regions, yellow predominates in the early stages and white becomes dominant later. The flowering period tends to be longer in the early stages in both temperate and tropical successions.

The increasing importance of animals in succession is associated with dispersal too. Species with small gravity- and wind-dispersed seeds tend to be common in the early stages but are soon replaced by animal-dispersed ones, though species with hooked fruits or sticky seeds are also important early on. Winged seeds or fruits are typical of many lianes and very tiny wind-dispersed seeds are characteristic of many epiphytes. The large gravity-dispersed seeds tend to be common among the 'emergent' trees while species with explosive fruits are rather rare at any stage. There seem to be correlations between very tiny, very large and winged seeds with the increasing height of the canopy.

In summary, early successional plants tend to have flowers pollinated by wind or by small animals, fruits with many small seeds (and some forms of inbreeding), while mature canopy trees may tend to have large flowers pollinated by large animals, large fleshy fruits with few large seeds (and some form of outbreeding). Understorey plants in mature forest might be expected to have smaller flowers and pollinators and to have fruits with a greater number of smaller seeds. As with all generalizations in ecology, which makes it the despair of some scientists and the fascination of others, there are numerous exceptions to all of these.

4.7 Primary successions

In Malesia, the island of Jarak, 64 km from the Malayan coast, is believed to have lost its entire flora some 34 000 years ago when an eruption in Sumatra, some 224 km away, covered it in ash. By 1953, there were in the 40 ha area of the island only 93 species of angiosperms, all but thirteen of which seem to have been dispersed thither by animals. Of the rest, eight are thought to have been dispersed by sea, two by man and only three by wind: two orchids with minute seeds and one *Hoya* (Asclepiadaceae) with plumed ones (7).

When Krakatoa erupted in 1883, it is believed that all living things on it were killed: ash was deposited to an average depth of 30 m. Although it lies about 40 km from both Java and Sumatra, nine typical littoral plant species and a number of unidentified fruits were recorded from its shores within three years. Inland were several ferns, Compositae, grasses and other higher plants besides quantities of blue-green algae. By 1897, the littoral vegetation was very well developed and there was a rich grassland inland. Nine years later, the coastal vegetation closely resembled that of Java and, inland, there were pockets of scrub, though still a predominance of grassland. In 1908, there were stands of typical secondary forest trees such as species of *Macaranga* behind the beach vegetation, and by 1919 the grassland was changing into a *Macaranga-Ficus* (fig) woodland.

By 1934, the number of species recorded was 271 but, in 1979, although the number of species still seemed to be rising, a number of the earlier plant species could not be found, suggesting some turnover of species. Furthermore, the forest seemed to be held at a late secondary forest stage, representing a kind of truncated succession in the absence of a source of propagules of later successional species (24). The inability of propagules of typically late successional species to reach islands even so close to the mainland is even more clearly seen in truly oceanic islands, where only groups of plants with small or long-lived propagules can colonize and diversify (3, 25). Similarly, truncated successions have been recorded from the isolated cloud forests of northern Colombia in a model study by Sugden (26) who argues that the differences between these montane floras which are poor in endemics are due partly to chance.

There have been suspicions that some of the organisms on Krakatoa survived the eruption there and that many were later brought in by man. A recent study on a newly-created island which resulted from an eruption in a lake on an island off the north-east coast of New Guinea (27) showed better monitoring. The island of Motmot lies some 3 km from the nearest land and was surveyed several times between its eruption in 1968 and subsequent eruption and devastation of most of the flora in 1973. By 1972 there were 14 higher plant species, predominantly sedges, most of them probably carried to the island ectozoically by black ducks. Of the fauna, many strand beetles, ants and bugs are thought to have arrived on drifting organic matter, but there were also ants, earwigs and spiders as well as other invertebrates associated with algal crusts around the crater pond. Despite their being carnivorous, the spiders had already colonized by 1969 and it is interesting to note that this is paralleled in other biomes for it is spiders that are some of the earliest animal colonists of spoil tips in South Wales.

Non-mycorrhizal plants, such as sedges, tend to perpetuate on poor soils as there are no mycorrhizae to allow other species to get established unless fungal propagules are introduced at the same time as the seeds of their hosts (9). In primary successions of the type discussed here, this is unlikely because of the poor dispersability of vesicular-arbuscular fungi. It may well be that such fungi are dispersed only by rodents or by movement of soil by wind or water for, in the tropics, spore production is low. Other formations without such mycorrhizae are certain savanna types and vegetation maintained by fire.

The features of succession in tropical moist habitats contrast with those in drier ones. In these latter, the cycles are usually simpler and frequently involve coppicing of old stumps. In very wet forests in swamps, both freshwater and marine, the system may be very simple, too. For example, in mangroves in the New World, the succession is simply from *Acrostichum* fern stands to mangrove forest. It would seem easier to manipulate such systems than to manipulate the complexity of rain forest and, indeed, disturbance of rain forest may lead to the invasion of other vegetation types from harsher regimes such as drier forest or from higher altitudes. Furthermore, the introduction of early successional trees from such harsher environments could have a serious effect on the native vegetation, much as the introduction of *Eucalyptus* (Myrtaceae) and *Hakea* (Proteaceae) from Australia and of exotic pines has adversely affected the extremely rich ecosystems of the Cape region of Africa.

CHAPTER FIVE

THE COMPONENTS OF DIVERSITY

That it was possible in the last chapter to be able to discuss tropical rain forest dynamics in general is a result of the remarkable structural similarities between the rain forests of the three great tropical regions. Nevertheless, floristically, they differ greatly, which would indicate that the components of these remarkably similar-looking forests have evolved in parallel and in isolation.

The rain forests of the Far East are dominated by dipterocarps and their biology, for at their maximum, these may make up 80 % of emergent trees and 40 % of the understorey, whereas in Africa there is only a handful of species in a different subfamily, and in South America, just one recently described species. (This is placed in its own subfamily but is of somewhat enigmatic relationships and possibly represents the direct descendants of a line which existed before the families allied to Dipterocarpaceae were as recognizably distinct as they seem to be today).

In all three blocks of rain forest, by contrast, there are emergent legumes: for example *Mora* in the New World, *Koompassia* in Asia and *Cynometra* in Africa. Sometimes closely related genera are found in the same stages of the rain-forest cycle in different regions, such as *Cecropia* in America and *Musanga* in Africa (Moraceae, *sensu lato*), pioneers both, while other closely allied genera may have diverged in their ecology so that *Xylocarpus* is a genus of mangrove, sandy shores and rocky headlands in East Africa and eastwards in the Old World; *Carapa* is a swamp-forest genus in both America and Africa (Meliaceae). Within the same family, distinct but closely allied genera are found on either side of the Pacific—

53

Cedrela and *Guarea* in the Americas (the second also in Africa), *Toona* and *Dysoxylum* in Asia. Remarkable amphipacific affinities may occur at the species level, as in Chrysobalanaceae where the single Asiatic species of *Maranthes*, a largely African genus, is also recorded from Panama. Rarely though does the same species occur in two or more continents. Notable, in the same family, is *Chrysobalanus icaco* on either side of the Atlantic and *Ceiba pentandra* (Bombacaceae) in all three tropical regions: though not native in Indomalesia it has been long introduced there.

5.1 Geographical diversity

5.1.1 *Flora*

A glance at Table 2 shows the parallelisms in different types of forest

Table 2 Examples of families and genera containing dominant, abundant, conspicuous or subendemic woody plants in the major rain-forest regions with their main groups of epiphytes and secondary forest trees (largely from K. A. Longman and J. Jeník, *Tropical Forest and its Environment*, Longman, London, 1974, pp. 70–2).

Neotropics	Leguminosae	*Andira, Apuleia, Dalbergia, Dinizia, Hymenolobium, Mora*
	Sapotaceae	*Manilkara, Pradosia*
	Meliaceae	*Cedrela, Swietenia*
	Euphorbiaceae	*Hevea*
	Myristicaceae	*Virola*
	Moraceae	*Cecropia, Ficus*
	Lecythidaceae	*Bertholletia*
	Epiphytes	ferns, Orchidaceae, Bromeliaceae, Cactaceae
	Secondary	*Cecropia, Miconia, Vismia*
Africa	Leguminosae	*Albizia, Brachystegia, Cynometra, Gilbertiodendron*
	Sapotaceae	*Afrosersalisia, Chrysophyllum*
	Meliaceae	*Entandrophragma, Khaya*
	Euphorbiaceae	*Macaranga, Uapaca*
	Moraceae	*Chlorophora, Ficus, Musanga*
	Sterculiaceae	*Cola, Triplochiton*
	Ulmaceae	*Celtis*
	Epiphytes	ferns, Orchidaceae
	Secondary	*Harungana, Macaranga, Musanga*
Indomalesia	Dipterocarpaceae	*Dryobalanops, Hopea, Shorea*
	Leguminosae	*Koompassia*
	Meliaceae	*Aglaia, Dysoxylum*
	Moraceae	*Artocarpus, Ficus*
	Anacardiaceae	*Mangifera*
	Dilleniaceae	*Dillenia*
	Thymelaeaceae	*Gonystylus*
	Epiphytes	ferns, Orchidaceae, Asclepiadaceae, Rubiaceae
	Secondary	*Glochidion, Macaranga, Mallotus, Melastoma*

component in the three forest blocks. Remarkable are the epiphytes, for all continents have orchids and ferns but America alone has bromeliads (the one African species of this family is not an epiphyte) and, with the exception of species of the genus *Rhipsalis*, all the cacti. In Indomalesia there are epiphytes in Rubiaceae and Asclepiadaceae.

An analysis of the African flora as a whole by Thorne (1) showed that there were some 500 species of plant found on both sides of the tropical Atlantic, representing *c*.0.63% of the total. Of these, some 108 are restricted to West Africa and South America and 45 of those are aquatic, or more or less so, many others are from maritime or brackish habitats or are riparian, while yet others are thought to be human introductions. Some are real forest plants and have small seeds (like the orchids) or are thought to be bird-dispersed. Amphipacific affinities, extraordinarily, are much stronger, with higher numbers of families and of genera shared between America and Asia than between America and Africa, though, less surprisingly perhaps, the affinity between the floras of Africa and Asia is strongest of all. By comparison with Africa, the forests of Madagascar, now largely destroyed and covered with secondary *savoka* vegetation with introduced genera like *Melia* and *Psidium* (Myrtaceae), have a greater number of endemic families and many endemic genera, even of palms, a family in which Africa is notably poor (2).

5.1.2 Fauna

Some vertebrates   Similar parallelisms and differences are found when the fauna is compared (3). Although the forest avifauna of Africa is poorer than the Neotropical, the numbers of mammal species are similar, though there are more bat species in America. There are remarkable ecological counterparts (Fig. 6) in the two regions, particularly striking in ungulates and rodents. In the Costa Rica forests, there are populations of relatively sedentary seed- and fruit-eaters, notably agoutis and paras, which have no analogue in Malesia, however. Janzen suggests this may reflect the periodic, rather than continuous, fruiting of the major trees, the dipterocarps discussed below, and that, in turn, it may explain why the number of raptors is low. In general, species diversity is high, population density low and related species have differences in times of activity, food specialization and preferences for different levels in the forest. Mixed troops of monkeys are found though, apparently affording protection, while the members of different species maintain their own food preferences.

A far higher percentage of the non-flying mammal species of tropical

Figure 6   Morphological convergences among African (left) and neotropical (right) rain-forest mammals. From top to bottom and left to right: pygmy hippopotamus and capybara; African chevrotain and paca; royal antelope and agouti, yellowback duiker and brocket deer; terrestrial pangolin and giant armadillo. Members of each pair of animals are drawn to the same scale. Reproduced with permission from F. Bourlière in B. J. Meggers, E. S. Ayensu and D. Duckworth, *Tropical Forest Ecosystems in Africa and South America: a Comparative Review* (Smithsonian Inst., Washington, 1973).

rain forest is arboreal than is the case in temperate regions. For example, in Borneo the figure is 45 %, in Virginia, U.S.A., 15 %. Food is available in the form of buds, leaves, flowers and fruits so that bats, primates and rodents occur in the canopy, as do American sloths and African hyraxes and a number of insectivores and carnivores. Although the biomasses of arboreal and ground-living mammals are estimated to be about the same, the latter are represented by fewer individuals, for they are large or medium-sized ungulates, feeding on the scanty foliage, fallen fruits, roots and so on or grazing in glades and along riverbanks, or they are rodents, shrews and a few strictly terrestrial carnivores. There are no true fossorial mammals, possibly due to the wet nature of the soil, little litter and few worms. Although there are herds of buffalo, sounders of pigs and so on, most non-arboreal mammals are solitary, whereas the arboreal animals may be solitary, in family groups or troops, or continuously wandering and coalescing with others.

Amongst the birds, frugivores tend to be found in the higher reaches of the forest, the conspicuous ones being the hornbills in the Old World and the toucans in the New, and insectivores found lower down.

A summary of the birds and mammals has been provided by Whitmore in his *Tropical Rain Forests of the Far East*, where six 'communities' are recognized: (1) above-canopy—insectivorous and otherwise carnivorous birds and bats; (2) top-of-canopy—birds and mammals feeding largely on leaves and fruits but also nectar or insects; (3) middle-of-canopy flying animals, predominantly insectivorous birds and bats; (4) middle-of-canopy mammals which range up and down tree trunks from crown to ground level, largely mixed feeders and a few carnivores; (5) large ground-living herbivores and their carnivores; (6) small ground- or undergrowth-dwelling animals with varied diets from the forest floor, largely insectivorous or mixed feeders. In short, the top of the canopy is mostly occupied by primary consumers, the other habitats by fewer primaries and more secondaries.

Insects Insects tend to be concentrated within the canopy, though some show bimodality in their vertical distribution (4), occurring conspicuously at ground level as well. The vertical distribution of these animals may be obscured in regions of deeply dissected topography. Some insects have specific 'insular' habitats occupied by their larvae. Such are the mosquitoes, and biting midges found in the reservoirs of bromeliad plants in the New World or the pitchers of *Nepenthes* in the Old, which, like the cups formed by the bases of teasel leaves (*Dipsacus* spp.) in temperate countries, hold a mass of rotting organic materials, which the saprophagous larvae consume. Their predators are associated with them and, in *Nepenthes*, both seem to be immune to the digestive enzymes which convert other animals into absorbable materials for the plant.

There are geographical differences in insect distribution too. Bees, which are important pollinators for many tropical plants (see Chapter 7) are not evenly distributed (3). Unlike many tropical groups, the bees are well represented by species in temperate regions. They are best represented in the tropics of South America, less well in Africa and least in the Indomalesian region, the palaeotropical bee fauna thus becoming poorer in an easterly direction. There appears to be no close relationship between the number of bee species in an area and the number of species of angiosperms; for example, the Cape region of southern Africa, though rich in plant species, does not have particularly high numbers of bee species.

Biomass There are rather few measurements of the overall biomass of rain-forest animals, though estimates, probably not wrong by more than a factor of two (3), in Amazonia *terra firme* are 210 kg per ha, compared with only 64 for mangrove forest. This is much smaller than the ungulates and other vertebrates of African grasslands, estimated at 100–300 kg per ha, although the bulk of the biomass there as well as in the rain forest is in the soil fauna.

The animals depend ultimately on the vegetable framework of the forest and much of the following discussion will therefore be devoted to a consideration of some of the principal features of the trees and, to a lesser extent, the other plant forms in tropical rain forest.

5.2 Morphological diversity

5.2.1 *Tree form*

H. C. Dawkins concluded that despite the variation in taxonomic terms of the rain forest of different continents, it was reasonable to argue that a mature forest has a mean basal area, that is to say a total bole cross-sectional area, of 32 m^2 per ha and that where lower figures were found, as they were in Ghana, this could be attributed to major human disturbance (5). Few of the boles, though, have a girth of more than a metre, and none is as tall as the redwoods of California or the big gums (*Eucalyptus*) of Australia.

Figure 7   The trunk and crown of *Shorea leprosula*, a common dipterocarp of Borneo. Note the honey-gatherers' ladder.

Emergents and canopy species   Most of the forests have conspicuous emergents and some of them are of great commercial value. Such are the dipterocarps of south-east Asia and the Meliaceae of tropical West Africa, but these seldom exceed 50 m. The tallest angiosperm measured was the legume, *Koompassia excelsa*, which was 83.82 m tall in Sarawak. The only other rain-forest tree which has been shown to be taller was a specimen of *Araucaria hunsteinii* which attained 88.9 m in New Guinea. For comparison, the tallest tree grown in Britain is a noble fir, *Abies grandis* from North America, which had attained 58 m in 1980.

The taller forests are found in areas with an alternation of humid and drier seasons with a total precipitation of some 2000 mm and with well-drained soils. High precipitation areas with little seasonality have lower forests with impeded drainage. In the Amazon, then, the canopy may be at about 30–40 m with the emergent *Mora* and the Brazil nut, *Bertholletia excelsa*, reaching some 50 m, while in Indomalesia the emergent *Dryobalanops aromatica* and other dipterocarps may reach 60 m (Fig. 7). Contrasting with early-successional trees, the emergents have sympodially-branched hemispherical crowns. Indeed most of the canopy trees have sympodial crowns too, with shiny scleromorphic leaves with stomata almost confined to the lower surface. The crowns do not overlap and light may pass between them to juveniles below.

The sheer height of the canopy above the ground has meant that investigations of the biology of the trees and the other plants and animals associated with them are difficult to carry out using conventional methods. Mere collecting of specimens for herbaria may require the felling of a tree, the use of a gun to snipe off branches or the use of tree climbers, human or simian, to collect specimens. Most studies, though, require access to the canopy and a whole range of towers, ladders, platforms, ropewebs, walkways, hoists, balloons and even helicopters have been designed or employed in rain-forest studies (6).

Many trees, including dipterocarps, generally flower only when they have reached the canopy. Although in cultivation these may do so when five years old, they set no fruit. Precocious flowering is recorded in many tropical plants including *Citrus*, *Swietenia* and *Melia*, where it may occur in the seedling stage. Manipulation of *Triplochiton* (*obeche*) seedlings with hormones has resulted in precocious flowering and accelerated breeding programmes.

Architecture   As was outlined in Chapter 1, there are features other than height which mark out tropical rain forest. A consideration of the

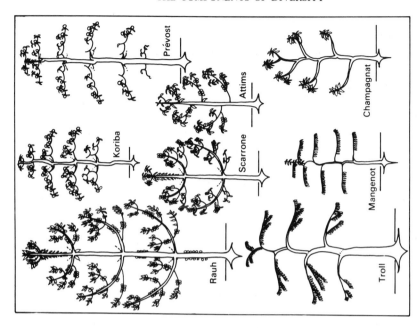

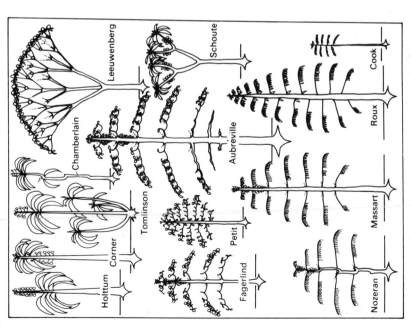

Figure 8 'Architectural models' of tropical trees as proposed by F. Hallé and R. A. A. Oldeman and named after other botanists. Root systems stylized; shoot systems in one plane, showing position and frequency of branching, branch orientation and inflorescence position. Reproduced with permission from P. B. Tomlinson in P. B. Tomlinson and M. H. Zimmermann (eds.), *Tropical Trees as Living Systems*, Fig. 7.1. (Cambridge University Press, 1978).

morphological, as contrasted with the taxonomic, variation in the trees themselves has led to a system of categorizing plant *architecture*, a field pioneered by Hallé and Oldeman. By considering the behaviour and fate of meristems, twenty or so *models*, or construction blueprints, for tree structures have been described and are most easily recognized in juvenile trees (Fig. 8). Of these, only three or four are commonly found in trees of temperate forests where there may be even fewer models represented, but an array of other models may be found in the herbaceous flora of temperate vegetation. The models are found in a wide range of sizes so that it may seem rather difficult to associate any particular model with an 'ecological strategy'. Nevertheless, taking tropical trees, it is sometimes possible to see trends. Although these models are referred to as distinct, there are intermediates and it is preferable to think of the models as particularly frequently expressed parts of an architectural continuum (7).

In the simplest model (Holttum) the tree is unbranched and the single meristem is destroyed in producing a massive terminal inflorescence. This is found in some palms, such as the talipot, *Corypha umbraculifera*, which after 50–70 years of vegetative growth produces an inflorescence 5–6 m tall and 10 m across and then fruits, flooding the surroundings with seeds. In dicotyledonous trees, this is rarer, but occurs, for example, in species of *Spathelia* (Rutaceae) in the American tropics. In *Corypha*, about 15 % of the total dry matter is converted into seeds and, although the time scale is different, it behaves like the annual or biennial herbs familiar in the vegetable garden (lettuce, carrot or parsnip) in this respect. It is argued that the production of masses of seed at rather irregular intervals in any particular place may have the effect of swamping the seed 'predators' with plenty. The increase in predator population lags behind, and so by the time it has increased the uneaten seeds would have germinated and thus escaped. Other unbranched trees, like most palms, have lateral inflorescences which do not herald the death of the tree. This form of architecture (Corner) is known in 39 families of flowering plants as well as tree ferns and several fossil groups (8) and occurs commonly in treelets of the forest floor. Compared with the first model, it is rare in herbs and, in the temperate zones possibly the most familiar are the plantains, *Plantago* spp. (Plantaginaceae). Both models have a variation (Tomlinson), where suckers are formed, repeating the main axis, giving rise to clumps or groups of plants linked by stolons. This is the most familiar model of architecture in perennial herbs in temperate countries and is the stuff of herbaceous borders. Many palms do this, as do cultivated bananas and their relation the 'Traveller's Palm' of Madagascar, *Ravenala madagascari-*

Figure 9 *Polyscias kikuyuensis* (Araliaceae), a fastgrowing 'ivy-tree' with Leeuwenberg's Model, in the montane forest of northwest Kenya.

ensis (Musaceae), a species in secondary *savoka*, where it is a pioneer. It is possible that such clumps promote a relatively closed nutrient system (7).

None of these simple models which, in trees, include massive buds and leaves (pachycaul), is found in temperate trees, unlike one where the innovations arise from aerial parts of the plant after the death of the meristem in flowering. This model (Leeuwenberg) is represented by the sumach, *Rhus typhina* (Anacardiaceae), a fast-growing treelet of gardens, native to North America. After each flowering, successive tiers of branches and leaves are formed so that several orders of branching are achieved. With branching, the new twigs are successively smaller, as are the leaves. Although in cultivation this can be reversed by taking cuttings and starting the plant again, as in the frangipani, *Plumeria alba* (Apocynaceae), it leads in the forest to a rather short-lived tree. It is the common construction of a number of *Solanum* and other species like *Manihot esculenta* (cassava) and *Ricinus communis* (castor oil) in the early stages of succession. It is not always associated with such an 'r-strategy', to use a zoological parallel, i.e. with rapid growth, short life-cycle and the production of many offspring, for this model is to be found in the slow-growing pachycaul giant groundsels of the afro-alpine belt of the Central and East African mountains (9).

As can be seen from Fig. 8, there is a wide range of form in branched trees, some with marked stratification into a tiered form, 'pagoda trees'. These, like most of the models, occur in a wide range of families; in other words, models are *grades* of construction, attained in parallel in divers groups of plants. The pagoda form is sometimes associated with pollination or dispersal by bats, but it represents one of a number of models which can present a multilayered canopy to incoming radiation. Horn (10) has shown that such a system is more drought-resistant than a mono-layer system. The explanation lies in the fact that for every unit of incident radiation there are more layers and therefore a greater leaf area for the dissipation through transpiration of the energy not used in photosynthesis. Therefore the mean water-loss per unit of photosynthetic area is less. These layers allow light through, and therefore other plants can become established below them. In this way, shade-bearers can become established under the multilayers so that there is a correlation between multilayers and early successional trees.

The monolayers cast a dense shade and nothing, not even their own offspring, may develop beneath them in extreme cases. Such trees in Europe or North America are the beeches (*Fagus*) and it is estimated that some 20–30 % of all trees have this model (Troll), which seems to be able to exhibit great plasticity (7). Oaks, compared with their allies, the beeches, have upward-pointing twigs with spirally arranged leaves (Rauh) rather than weeping branches with leaves presented distichously. Oaks have a rich undergrowth of herbs and shrubs: the forest floor beneath beeches is inimicable to almost all plants, save a few saprophytes. In temperate trees, such contrasts are found between the allied willows and poplars and within genera in both the temperate and tropical regions. The two types of architecture therefore represent just the end of the range of tree form found in the tropics.

Reiteration Juveniles have thin branches which can be lost, but mature trees do not lose major axes so readily, since the apical dominance of the leader is then also lost. (Some tree families, e.g. Annonaceae and Lauraceae, seem not to undergo this 'metamorphosis'). As they grow up, however, trees may suffer smashed limbs from a variety of causes—insect and fungal attack and grazing from animals, such as orang-utans for example, which may break off branches to get at their food. After such damage, some trees may never recover (some palms are an example), but generally speaking buds grow out and repeat the basic model of the species, a phenomenon known as reiteration. This is also manifest in coppice shoots or root suckers, just as in the suckering forms of the simpler trees.

Most trees differ from the simple models set out in detail above in that not all the branch units or 'articles' are equivalent to one another. In the sumach, as in cassava or castor oil, they are, but in most trees there is a 'division of labour' between the branches (specializing in photosynthesis) and the trunk (in support), as in rubber, avocado pear, coffee, cocoa or mahogany. Some trees have meristems which give rise to axes which are mixed, that is they give rise to trunk and branch portions, their orientation changing with development. This is the form in beech and elm and many tropical legumes. With age, all such trees reach a maximum, whereafter they merely replace pieces lost, reiterating the model in an essentially herbaceous way only. The result is the range of crown form characteristic of different species: the thick, dense crowns of *Mangifera* (mango, Anacardiaceae) compared with the light crowns of many legumes for example.

Other variable features Variation is found in other features. Bark may be black, as in some *Diospyros* species (ebonies), to white through red-brown, but, at the forest edge, barks are often bleached pale grey. They may be smooth or fissured or scaly, sometimes with spectacular strips or patches

Figure 10 Buttresses of *Koompassia excelsa* (Leguminosae) in northern Borneo. Note relative size of man.

falling away. The smooth barks are slow-growing. The trunks may be fluted or fenestrated as in some Rubiaceae, while the fluting at ground level is often continued into buttresses which spread out from the bole. These may be long and sinuous or may be some metres tall, concave or convex (Fig. 10). They certainly increase the soil-surface area covered by the tree and may, therefore, make it more stable. Indeed, there is a certain degree of correlation: emergents with deep taproots having no such buttresses and *vice versa*. A negative correlation between bark thickness and buttressing has been found in trees of lower montane forest on Dominica in the West Indies (11).

Stilt-roots, that is roots arising from the trunk above ground-level and eventually reaching the ground, where they reiterate, are characteristic of many monocotyledonous trees such as *Pandanus* (Pandanaceae) and palms. In some palms, the base of the trunk may wither, so that the tree is supported on a polypodal arrangement of the stilt-roots. In *Socratea exorrhiza*, a palm of the Peruvian Amazon (12), such roots may allow the plant to 'move' away from behind or under obstacles. Some species do not produce the stilt-roots if grown in dry conditions. Similarly, pneumatophores or 'breathing roots', characteristic of certain swamp species (Fig. 11), may not develop under dry conditions. This is a well-known phenomenon in the temperate swamp-cypress. *Taxodium distichum*, which has 'knee-roots', commonly seen in mangrove swamps. The two closely allied *Xylocarpus* species (Meliaceae), which grow together in such swamps in Malesia, can be distinguished from one another by only one having pneumatophores, so that their function is not readily explained.

Aerial roots occur in other conditions, as anyone who grows the 'Swiss cheese plant', the Mexican *Monstera deliciosa* (Araceae), knows, for this is a scrambling and climbing aroid, which roots in pockets of humus in tree crowns. Roots may be found growing into the humus collecting in the persistent leaf-bases of tree-ferns or other trees.

5.2.2   Other growth forms

Stranglers and other epiphytes   The most spectacular roots are probably those of the strangling figs, plants which begin as epiphytes and eventually, by producing roots down the host trunk to the ground and by the production of a crown, shading out the host's crown, sometimes completely engulf and exterminate the host, leaving the figs as free-standing trees. Such stranglers occur in unrelated genera besides the figs: in *Spondias* (Anacardiaceae, Philippines); *Fagraea* (Loganiaceae) and *Timonius*

Figure 11 'Knee-roots' or pneumatophores of *Lophopetalum multinervium* (Celastraceae) in the swamp forests of northern Borneo.

(Rubiaceae) both in Papuasia; *Clusia* (Guttiferae) and *Coussapoa* (Urticaceae) in the New World; but also *Metrosideros* (Myrtaceae) in New Caledonia and New Zealand; *Wightia* (Scrophulariaceae), and possibly *Schefflera* (Araliaceae); while some epiphytes, like some of the woody lobelioids peculiar to the Hawaiian forests, may have some of the effects of these stranglers. Indeed, the division between stranglers, epiphytes, climbers and scramblers becomes confused. Furthermore, some epiphytes may have the effect of parasites without physically penetrating the living tissues of their hosts: the small fern, *Pyrrosia nummulariifolia*, is a pest of coffee in that it webs the twigs and is believed to cause their rotting. The hemi-parasites in the Loranthaceae (*sensu lato*) allied to mistletoe, *Viscum album*, are a common feature of tropical forests and may bear hyper-parasites of the same family, even to the second degree.

Vascular epiphytes often have small seeds, as was explained in Chapter 4, and are usually xeromorphic. They often have crassulacean acid metabolism, again a feature of plants adapted to dry habitats, and some of them have unorthodox modes of nutrient supply. Perhaps the most remarkable are the ant-plants, *Hydnophytum* and *Myrmecodia* (Rubiaceae), of the Malesian forests. Through labelling experiments (13) it has been established that ants bring nutrients into the chambered tuber of these plants and that these nutrients are absorbed by the host. In *Hydnophytum*, there is an aperture produced by the plant, whereas, in the New World, ants chew an entry into their host bromeliad, *Tillandsia medusae* (14). Furthermore, it is now known that some epiphytic orchids have fungi in the cortex of their roots and that these are linked thus to the rotting host. Curiously, then, the claim of a 'parasitic' nature of orchids, long-advocated by foresters and denied by botanists, has some substance.

Lianes, saprophytes and more parasites   Although some climbers cannot be absolutely distinguished from epiphytes in the broad sense, lianes are very numerous and may make up 40 % of the total flora, in terms of species numbers, in some forests. They may have clinging roots or hooks and, indeed, most are hoisted into the canopy by their hosts and are able to extend internodally when apparently mature, thereby compensating for any growth by their hosts which might otherwise cause them to fracture.

A remarkable root-climber is the orchid, *Galeola altissima* of Java, which is a saprophyte and alleged to grow to 40 m, though usually less. Other, herbaceous, saprophytes in the forest include species of several pantropical genera of rather bizarre appearance. They are often con-spicuous on the forest floor for being white, bright yellow or pale blue. The fruiting bodies of saprophytic fungi are not frequently encountered as they are very seasonal.

Of parasites, the most celebrated are the Malesian *Rafflesia* spp., some of the most remarkable of all angiosperms, living entirely within the tissue of certain vines except when in flower. The flowers may reach 1 m in diameter, though the plants are rare and some species are now threatened with extinction. There are root-parasites in the Balanophoraceae, again with brightly coloured but morphologically much reduced flowering shoots, throughout the tropics. The only 'herbaceous' gymnosperm is a shrubby parasite, which is parasitic on its close allies in the Podocarpaceae of New Caledonia.

Herbs   By comparison with the richness of the canopy, the herbaceous flora of the forest floor is often rather species-poor and the most commonly encountered families are the relatively 'advanced' dicotyledonous ones like Rubiaceae, Gesneriaceae, Acanthaceae or monocotyledons, notably Zingiberaceae, Araceae, Marantaceae and Commelinaceae. The grasses there tend to have rather broad leaves and are considered rather primitive in the family as a whole. The coloured leaves of some forest herbs have been alluded to in Chapter 2, while many of the dicotyledons have 'bumps' on either side of the main vein, which may possibly act like drip-tips in the drainage of the leaf.

The form of rain forest herbs varies more than does that of temperate ones (15). Some, like Zingiberaceae, have rhizomes, often long-stoloniferous giving scattered clumps, but rather like temperate herbs. Others form patches from the stems becoming decumbent and rooting, as in *Cyrtandra* (Gesneriaceae), many Urticaceae and species with lateral inflorescences. Those with terminal inflorescences, as many Acanthaceae, shoot from buds after flowering: these may either be basal or grow out nearer the top of the plant, which is not found in temperate herbs to any great extent. Others are like the unbranched treelets with lateral inflorescences, e.g. *Sonerila* (Melastomataceae) and *Neckia* (Ochnaceae). On vertical faces, the rosette of leaves may be asymmetric, the lower leaves being the larger, up to 70 cm in *Cyrtandra mirabilis*, leaves which could not be held on the flat as they are very thin. The Gesneriaceae also include some plants which resemble a stalked leaf bearing flowers from the base of the lamina. Such organs are intermediate in structure between leaves and stems, terms indeed which are applicable to the majority of, but not all, higher plants.

Some herbs are hapaxanthic, i.e. they flower once and then die, such as *Strobilanthes* (Acanthaceae), and are often associated with more seasonal forests, as in India, or as *Mimulopsis* and *Isoglossa* of the same family are in Africa. In seasonal forests, there are true storage organs as in temperate corms, bulbs and tubers. There may be tubers or swollen storage trunks as in *Impatiens mirabilis* (Balsaminaceae) of the seasonal limestone forests of northern Malaya. In the seasonal forests of Africa, a species of the aroid, *Amorphophallus*, flowers and then produces leaves from its corm. In the scarcely seasonal Sarawak, however, *Amorphophallus* corms produce flowers in one year, leaves in another, though flowering seems to take place every few years, rather than every other year. It is perhaps unique amongst rain forest plants in having a well marked annual dormancy.

Rheophytes   A further category of plant forms, embracing both herbs and woody species, is that of the rheophytes, which are plants confined to the beds of fast-flowing rivers throughout the world. Two totally tropical

Figure 12   A cauliflorous durian (*Durio* sp., Bombacaceae) in Sarawak, Borneo.

families, the Podostemaceae and Hydrostachyaceae, which are small thalloid angiosperms growing on rocks, make up some half of the world total but, in all, some 60 different families of angiosperms include rheophytes. They usually have narrow leaves or leaflets and some tropical ones have seeds dispersed by fish (16).

5.2.3 'Anomalies'

Characteristics, which when seen in temperate floras are often referred to as 'anomalous', are in fact more typically tropical features of the forest, including cauliflory, as was mentioned in Chapter 1. This is the production of flowers from twigs, as they grow into trunks, or from long-dormant buds. There is frequently variation within this, so that young trees may have flowers borne in the leaf-axils or just behind them, older trees producing them from the major branches or from the bole. Sometimes the flowers and fruits are produced at ground level, while some figs (the so-called geocarpic ones) produce their inflorescences on long ground-level branches.

Figure 13   The cauliflorous *jak* fruit (*Artocarpus heterophyllus*, Moraceae) under cultivation in Tanzania.

Characteristic of some tree species is the production of flowers on the ends of very long inflorescences hanging like bell-ropes in the forest. Within species of the genus *Chisocheton* (Meliaceae) such ropes may be 7 m long (17) while others of the 51 species in the genus are cauliflorous, ramiflorous or even produce their flowers on the leaves. The inflorescences may be axillary or internodal. They may consist of determinate inflorescences or short shoots bearing such inflorescences. This genus is further remarkable for its leaves, which in some species are imparipinnate or paripinnate like the majority of species in the family, while in others only the juvenile foliage is like this but that of mature trees has crozier-like buds (pseudogemmulae) at the apex of the leaves. With succeeding flushes of the tree, more leaflets are produced from the pseudogemmula, the older ones falling off. Eventually this 'leaf' is dropped, when it can be seen that it has secondary depositions of xylem, like a stem. In short, these plants defy the pigeon-holing of temperate-trained morphologists. Indeed, these branch-like leaves behave, in the epiphyllous species, rather like the leaf-like branches of some Euphorbiaceae, such as species of *Phyllanthus* with their opposite leaves and deciduous branches.

5.3 Intraspecific variation

The variation within species of the plants which make up rain forest can be exposed only by intensive taxonomic studies and, although knowledge of the basis of this variation in tropical plants is still in a preliminary stage, there is now good documentation of the types of variation pattern to be seen in rain-forest species. Again, there are no clear-cut categories, but within any group intensively described, there are often to be found (1) species which are morphologically rather homogeneous, (2) species which may be more or less divisible into ecogeographically distinguishable races, usually labelled subspecies, and frequently (3) others which exhibit a form of variation absolutely intractable to the taxonomist and known as ochlospecies (18). In these latter, at any particular locality there may appear to be two distinct entities, differing in some clearly recognizable features. At a second locality, there may be two other such, but the four together begin to merge in characteristics, and so on. Such forms may represent speciation in progress and have often been labelled 'provenances' by foresters, though variously given specific, varietal or form rank or an informal classification by taxonomists (17). It cannot be expected that a rigid hierarchical system, demanded by nomenclature (or nomenclaturists), should encompass organisms absolutely, if we believe in evolution at all.

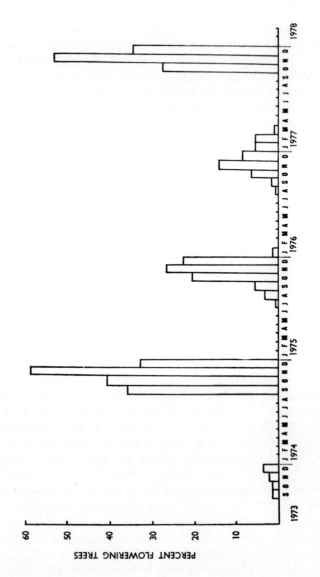

Figure 14 Percent flowering trees in five plots in Pasoh, Negri Sembilan, Malaysia, 1973–78. Reproduced with permission from S. K. Yap in *Malaysian Forester* **45** (1982) 23, Fig. 1.

5.4   Seasonal variation and other cycles

5.4.1   *Plant cycles*

Sex   The coming and passing of the seasons are such an accepted part of temperate living that the phenomena of flowering and fruiting seasons, leaf-fall and perennation seem the norm to temperate-trained biologists. In the Asiatic tropics, regular fruiting seasons are well known in such fruit trees as durians (*Durio zibethinus*, Bombacaceae), *lanseh* (*Lansium domesti-cum*, Meliaceae), mangosteens (*Garcinia mangostana*, Guttiferae) and so on, while the flowering of the *kechapi*, *Sandoricum koetjape* (Meliaceae), was formerly regarded as the cue for sowing rice in Malaya. This regular fruiting contrasts with the state of affairs in cultivated bananas (which are of complex ancestry and are triploid), pineapples and papaya which produce fruit almost all the year round in tropical countries.

Indeed, the regularly-fruiting fruit trees are exceptional. In lowland rain forest in West Malaysia (19), the phenology of the trees was recorded over a four-year period from a suspended transect walkway. Here, no strong seasonality was observable, though there appeared to be more species in flower after dry spells at whatever time of the year these occurred. Some 85 % of the species there did not flower or produce new leaves at regular intervals and, within species, there was a lack of synchrony. There seemed to be no clear relationship between the flowering trees and their dispersal agents, suggesting that these comprise a wide spectrum of generalists, depending on there being a considerable proportion of the tree species in flower at any one time. There are few species that flower continuously from youth to death. These include *Dillenia suffruticosa* in Malaysia, but again they are exceptional. In more seasonal forests, most flowering occurs at the end of the dry season so that water stress is invoked as a stimulus to flowering. On Barro Colorado Island, Panama, herbs in clearings, which are most sensitive to climatic change, flower at the beginning of the dry season while herbs in the forest proper flower during the rainy season and probably respond to intense rain following drought. Similarly, trees which usually flower in the wet season will flower in the dry if there is a period of heavy rain then (20).

Some plants are known to respond to cold periods by flowering, the most celebrated example being the pigeon orchid, *Dendrobium crumenatum*, again of Malaysia, which flowers nine days after such a cold snap. A number of commercial plants have been examined in detail, so that it is known that coffee (*Coffea arabica*, Rubiaceae) responds to heavy rainfall. Where slight seasonal differences in photoperiod exist, some plants seem to be able to respond by flowering like many temperate plants, e.g. *Hildegardia barteri* (Sterculiaceae) in West Africa. Locally 'bad' years for fruits may be due to heavy rains, which may affect or even kill the flowers and their pollinator. Some trees, on the other hand, flower very rarely and little is known of the phenology of the late-successional shade-bearers in this respect, but *Homalium grandiflorum* (Flacourtiaceae) in Malesia, for example, flowers once in only 10–15 years.

Mass flowering   In a five-year study of fruit trees in a lowland rain forest, again in Malaysia (21), two major peaks of flowering were observed (Fig. 14), although some species flowered annually as a population, the intensity varying year by year. Some, like the dioecious *Xerospermum noronhianum* ('*X. intermedium*', Sapindaceae) opened flowers over rather long periods on any one tree, thus promoting outcrossing over a long season. One of the peaks coincided with a mass flowering of the diptero-carps. Owing to the ecological (and commercial) importance of these latter trees, many ideas have been put forward as to the stimulus for flowering, which takes place heavily every 2–5 or sometimes 9–11 years on average. Ng (22) has made a convincing case for the stimulus in West Malaysia being a sharp increase in mean daily sunshine in January or February of the masting year. In years of such gregarious flowering, the percentage of trees producing good seed is highest while it is low in years of sporadic flowering and lowest of all when the number of trees flowering is least. These flowering pulses do not seem to be 'all-or-nothing' phenomena like the familiar phytochrome system, for a stronger stimulus will cause a more massive flowering response. In Borneo such flowering may occur through-out an area as large as Sabah, or may be confined to particular valleys. Because these flowerings do not take place in successive years, it would appear that a build-up of photosynthate must take place first. There is genetic variation in responding to the stimulus as there seems to be in the length of the flowering to fruiting periods of divers rain forest trees (23). This period may vary from year to year but, of 86 species examined in West Malaysia, 90 % had completed it in six months and all within a year.

   One of the many possible evolutionary explanations for the gregarious flowerings has been put forward by Janzen (24), who argues that the predation of the seeds may be heavy, the predators, particularly insects such as weevils, not being very specific about their food plants. He adds that such pressure may have been greater in the past in that dipterocarp seeds are now sought by pigs and man but possibly formerly by elephants and rhinoceros, now largely removed from the forests. Gregarious flowering within a species would swamp the predators, like the hapaxanthic *Corypha*, mentioned above. The flowering of individuals of other species coinciding with mass flowering of dipterocarps might promote greater survival of the seeds, so that a response similar to those in dipterocarps might be selected for. As a result, selection would favour a low animal density, generalists and nomadic behaviour.

The spectacularly long cycles of the reproductive behaviour of the bamboos, up to a century or more, is rather rare in the equatorial belt, though a similar explanation is sought for those. Janzen suggests that the 'counting' of so many years might be difficult in the tropics and the essential synchrony lost: in the more seasonal regions, where at least 200 species of bamboo flower gregariously, those plants which flower early or late are likely to be exterminated by predators, thus reinforcing the mass-flowering habit.

Vegetative growth: flushing and annual rings Vegetative growth in tropical plants is rarely continuous, as was pointed out in Chapter 1. The main peak of leaf growth, or *flushing*, in West Malaysia occurs after the driest time of the year and a second peak begins before, and extends into, the wettest period of the year. A few trees there, e.g. *Artocarpus lowii* (Moraceae), produce leaves continuously, but most produce one recognizable flush per year. *Terminalia catappa* (Combretaceae) has two flushes per annum though there is some infraspecific variation in this. In the more seasonal forests of Barro Colorado Island, *Tabebuia rosea* (Bignoniaceae) and *Quararibea asterolepis* (Bombacaceae) lose their leaves twice a year, and some *Ficus* spp. lose them several times (20). *Breynia cernua* in Java has a cycle of $5\frac{1}{2}$ months, *Delonix regia* some nine months and *Heritiera macrophylla* two years and eight months. Two flushes per annum are rare in canopy trees but up to seven flushes have been reported in juveniles.

Usually new leaves are produced as the old ones fall, like temperate evergreens, but some trees may become completely leafless, as in *Toona australis* (Meliaceae) and *Piptadeniastrum africanum* (Leguminosae), both large trees, and, indeed, deciduousness of this kind occurs in a higher percentage of trees in the emergents than lower in the forest. It is sometimes associated with flowering, making the flowers rather conspicuous. Sometimes new leaves are brightly coloured or speckled or may hang limp, as in the legumes *Brownea* of the New World and *Saraca* and *Amherstia* of the Old. These extend once the xylem in the stems and leaves has thickened. Withering leaves are sometimes startlingly coloured and may be diagnostic for allied plants, e.g. of the two common forms of

Sandoricum koetjape grown in West Malaysia, the leaves of one wither red, the other yellow (25).

The rhythmic nature of flushing has been closely investigated in rubber, *Hevea brasiliensis*, native to South America. It produces about six extensions a year and branching begins after about nine of these (7). Each branch behaves like the axis except that its branches tend to be on the lower side. This independent endogenous rhythm can be overcome by stress; for example, if most of the leaf laminas are removed, continuous growth follows. Tea (*Camellia sinensis*, Theaceae) has up to four flushes a year, a matter of some considerable commercial importance, as the commodity is prepared from the young shoots. For comparison, a deciduous temperate tree like sessile oak, *Quercus petraea*, has a rhythmic apical activity of 10–15 days, followed by 8–15 days of extension; in other words a 20–30 day cycle (but with winter dormancy, which needs a cold period to be broken, superimposed on this). Even in seasonal forests, leaf deciduousness is not universal, for it is seen to be related to nutrient status—a poorer status is associated with less deciduousness. Species may then behave differently under different conditions.

Of trees that produce leaves continuously, perhaps the most closely investigated have been palms, many but not all of which, as in the coconut, have a constant number of leaves in the bud, once the adult size is attained. In that species, the crown has 30 expanded and 30 expanding leaves, one expanding each month and one falling each month, so that the life of a leaf is five years.

A feature of trees associated with seasonality in temperate regions is the formation of *annual rings* in the secondary xylem, that is the juxtaposition of small, thick-walled, xylem elements at the end of a season with the large thin-walled elements at the beginning of the next. Not surprisingly, perhaps, these either do not occur in tropical trees or their periodicity is not fully understood. In temperate trees, a set-back such as defoliation may lead to the laying down of two rings in a season, but the rigid pattern of one ring per season, of such great value in dendrochronology and the correcting of radiocarbon dating, is a general and unique feature of such trees.

5.4.2   Animal cycles

A number, if not the majority, of rain-forest mammals breed seasonally and, in primates, there may possibly be a correlation between conception and the coolest time of the year (3). Animals in general, even insects, tend to have single offspring or broods when compared with their temperate allies. The small size but high frequency of broods may be an adaptation to a sustained yet small production of their food. Very few species of bird and probably no individuals (26) breed all year round, most species probably beginning to breed when food supplies increase after a lean period. This may differ from year to year and between insectivores, frugivores or nectarivorous species. Despite this, the post-breeding moult occurs at the same time every year. It has been argued that as adult survival is greater than in temperate birds, yet reproductive rate very much lower, and moult is an energy-demanding process, there may be as high a selection pressure for timing the moult in the tropical belt as there is for breeding seasonality in temperate birds.

There is a considerable interest in this field, particularly with respect to Amphibia and various insect groups, but there is no modern synthesis. Of Asiatic examples, frogs and lizards in Sarawak seem to show little seasonality, whereas soil invertebrates seem to increase with the fungal mycelia which burgeon in the wet period after dry spells. In southern peninsular Malaysia, for example, forest agaric fungi have two general 'fruiting' seasons in most years.

CHAPTER SIX

SPECIES RICHNESS

6.1 Speciation

Not only trees but almost all groups of animals and plants exhibit their greatest variety in the tropics (1) in terms of the number of species recorded there. How is it that the tropics generate, or at least harbour, so many species and how is it that these can coexist? The answer to the first question involves an analysis of speciation, which in turn leads to a consideration of the ecological conditions under which such speciation might have taken place, and the answer to the second also involves an analysis of the physical and biotic influences on the organisms concerned.

A prerequisite of speciation is variation, and if the variation patterns within species are examined, some ideas of the possible modes of incipient speciation may be gained. As was explained in Chapter 5, some tropical tree species seem to be very homogeneous in their morphology over wide ranges, even including populations widely separated from others with little possibility for gene exchange. Examples of this are species now in populations in southern India and far away in Malesia, like the yam ally *Trichopus zeylanicus* (Dioscoreaceae). Other species seem to be separable into geographical races based on their morphological features. These are usually given subspecific rank. The segregation may be more precisely ecological than geographical in (say) forest and savanna races of trees in Africa. Yet other species exhibit variation patterns that defy analysis of the sophistication of present-day biology. Such are the ochlospecies (p. 73) of White, a term coined to convey the annoyance such species cause

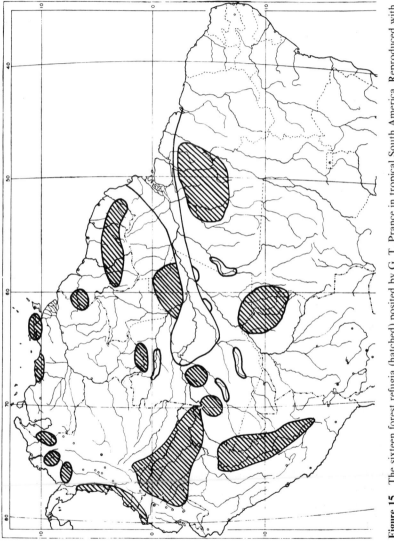

Figure 15 The sixteen forest refugia (hatched) posited by G. T. Prance in tropical South America. Reproduced with permission from *Acta amazonica* **3**, 3 (1973) 23, Fig. 24.

taxonomists, and including some of the ebonies (*Diospyros* spp., Ebenaceae) of Africa.

Although there is much to be said in favour of the notion of evolution by discrete jumps in plants, particularly through allopolyploidy involving small numbers of individuals, current orthodoxy holds that the greater part of speciation events occurs through the isolation of fragments of an initial population, the change of these fragments in response to the conditions in their isolation and, with the breakdown of isolation, the co-existence of the newly speciated populations in one locality. Clearly, many partially speciated populations will come together and then merge once more. The ochlospecies is not readily explained however, while apomixis is another phenomenon to be taken into account.

It is now generally argued that within the lowland Neotropics, the fragmentation of populations took place as a result of climatic and associated vegetational changes in the last two million years. The changes seem to have been alternating periods of humid conditions and aridity. It is argued that during the dry phases, the humid forests would have been fragmented into island-like refugia (Fig. 15) of isolated blocks of forest. The organisms would then come back into contact, merge again or coexist as new species. There is geomorphological evidence for such contractions, supported by palaeobotanical work (2). Much evidence comes from the mapping of the distributions of rain-forest organisms, most notable being those of various tree families by Prance and his co-workers. Although the detail of the distributions varies, the broad pattern is the same. Similar schemes have been drawn up for several mammalian groups, certain butterfly genera, various reptiles and amphibians while a good deal of work has been carried out on the distributions of the avifauna. All these give some idea of possible refugia, sometimes referred to as centres of dispersal. That the modern distributions of organisms could be explained in terms of ecological rather than historical factors has been rejected, for no clear-cut correlations between the distributions and any ecological factors such as precipitation or soil factors could be discerned.

6.2 Species diversity

A number of hypotheses to explain the coexistence of so many species has been proposed. Some place emphasis on biotic, others on environmental factors. Of biotic arguments for explaining greater tropical diversity, one of the most familiar is that there are more 'niches' than in temperate latitudes, arising from more habitats or more resources, but these hark back to environmental arguments ultimately. Usually, however, it is argued that there may be a finer division of these habitats or resources or, in short, that tropical species are more specialized. Added to this is the historical argument that in the tropics more of the available 'niches' are filled and that, because of ice ages or other environmental factors, temperate habitats are not yet saturated with species. Fundamental to the idea of finely divided 'niches', however, is the notion that there are finite or limiting resources, whereas in trees in the tropics with abundant light, water, CO_2 and a conservative nutrient-cycling system, this seems as inappropriate as it does in the case of tropical corals making up species-rich reefs, where food is not readily seen as limiting when compared with space to occupy. Another and very fashionable biotic argument is that of 'predation', that there are more predators and greater predation in the tropics than in temperate regions, and that these are matched by more defensive or avoidance mechanisms. The prevalence of predation appears to be correlated with the relative lack of seasonality, for in temperate countries, winters prevent a good deal of predation. Nevertheless, it would seem that this 'explanation' is merely a restatement of the facts of tropical high diversity in that if there are more species, there will be more species of predators.

Of environmental arguments, attention is focused on those features of the environment that are peculiar to the tropics. Firstly, the tropical belt is a large region and for marine organisms, for example, the sheer size of the available area for diversification is greater, though, as we have seen, tropical rain forest occupies only a small part of the tropical land-surfaces, and thus a very small fraction of the tropical global surface. Nevertheless, the range of environmental heterogeneity in the tropics from the foot of the Andes to their peaks is greater spatially than in temperate regions, even if the environment in temperate regions varies greatly temporally. We are left, furthermore, with the heterogeneity in the tropics engendered by disturbance through storms or other violent environmental factors such as fire and the seasonal changes of weather, some of which, like short droughts, are unpredictable. Cyclones are seen as a force which prevents the ecological succession of coral reefs from terminating in less species-rich assemblages (in those reefs, the earlier stages are more species-rich). Furthermore, the importance of predation can be seen as yet another element in the disturbance picture.

In summary, time, space, resources, competition and predation, may play a part in explaining the biological diversity of the tropics.

6.2.1   Environmental heterogeneity

What is the evidence for some microenvironmental differentiation of rain forest supporting a diversity of species, each in the case of trees with very specific requirements in terms of nutrients, soil-water content and so on? Firstly, individuals do not all occur randomly in a forest and often there is a good deal of clumping as we have already discussed. Furthermore, a monograph of any large tropical group will show varying degrees of recognition of the ecological requirements of different species. Of the 51 species of *Chisocheton* (Meliaceae), in Malesia for example, one species is restricted to peat-swamp forest and another to limestone, while in dipterocarps, *Shorea curtisii* is always found on ridges and slopes apparently associated with particular water relations in the forest. Similarly, in the *igapó* forests, that is those inundated by black or clear water, in Brazil, the species distributions are thought to reflect differential tolerance of flooding (3).

An example which pinpoints the problem was exposed when a map of all trees over 20 cm diameter at breast height in $\frac{1}{2}$ sq km of the semi-deciduous forest of Barro Colorado Island was made (4). It showed that most species are patchily dispersed, while many appear to be randomly distributed and a very few are uniformly distributed. Most of those that are clumped, however, are in groups not associated with the topography, while some species are restricted to particular kinds of site: *Ocotea skutchii*, for example, is always on slopes. In short, some heterogeneity and aggregations may have a physical explanation, others not.

The precise ecological requirements of dipterocarps in Indomalesia is most recognizable, and their local heterogeneity associated with physical factors most obvious, when fertility is fairly low. Furthermore, when 46 forest sites in Costa Rica were examined (5) it was also found that there was a negative correlation between soil nutrient availability and the richness of tree species. In other words the highest species richness was found under 'poor' growth conditions. Under very low nutrient conditions in general, however, species numbers are low as they are, contrariwise, under greenhouse competition experiments with high nutrient levels.

6.2.2   Biotic factors

Of the biotic explanations of how coexisting species avoid competition, some are based on time-sharing of animal agents. For example, over a season, six species of *Shorea* are visited in turn by species of thrips, which are believed to be their major pollinators. Thus with non-specific pollinators, competition is avoided and there is no problem of the build-up of pollinators at any one time of year to satisfy any one plant species. The problem comes with the first-flowering species. Possibly it is apomictic! Similar time-sharing is known in dispersal. In Trinidad, 19 species of the pioneering *Miconia* (Melastomataceae) fruit successively, providing fruit for dispersing birds throughout the year and staggered batches of seedlings which avoid interspecific competition (6). There could also be 'shiftwork' in other examples—in that there is a segregation of animals between night and day.

Biotic explanations for both clumping and diversity have been adduced. The habits of some animals lead to the deposition of many seeds in one place. This is especially noticeable with frugivorous bats which, in a dry forest in Costa Rica, produce seed shadows of a mixture of species around fruiting trees in which they roost (7). Again, agoutis in S.E. Peru (8) store fruits of *Astrocaryum*, a palm, in hoards, which may lead to clumped distribution as well as to the 'clumped' behaviour of white-lipped peccaries which in turn disinter this food. By contrast, it has been argued by Janzen that species-specific 'predation' of juveniles growing around their mother will lead to a progressive decline in density of successful saplings towards the mother. This might then account for the apparently non-environmentally controlled distribution pattern in which other species could insinuate themselves in the holes of the forest 'lattice' devoid of the first species. This has been extended in the case of specific fruit and seed predators to account for the frequency of dioecy in some forests. In dioecious species, regulated in numbers by such predators, a high level of gene exchange could be maintained by the presence of a number of male trees which would not be attractive to these predators.

There are certain general observations which might favour this predator argument. In chalk grassland in Britain, for example, the removal of grazers, such as rabbits or sheep, has a devastating effect on the fine-leaved bouncy turf rich in species. In a few years, the sward may become dominated by the coarse tussock-forming grass, *Brachypodium pinnatum*, and eventually the vegetation turns into some form of scrub and possibly woodland. On the other hand, an increase in grazing pressure leads to the elimination of all but a few very tough species. At the maximum plant-species diversity, the grazing lowers the competitive ability of certain species, allowing, under the same conditions of soil, aspect and so on, the coexistence of the smaller species which otherwise could not exist there. What is perhaps most remarkable about this grassland is that it is only

D

maintained under active management—even rabbits were introduced by the Normans—and, although it resembles some periglacial assemblages of plants, it must have been reconstituted after the forest maximum unless there were extensive grazed glades in that period. In short, it is possibly not very old.

A series of observations first put together by Gillett (9) is perhaps nearer our subject. It is well known that it is difficult to grow plantation rubber (*Hevea brasiliensis*, originally from Brazil) successfully in the forest lands where that species grows wild, and it grows best in Malaysia; cocoa, which is also native to the New World, grows best in West Africa, cloves from Indonesia, in Zanzibar, and so on. The argument runs that in the absence of their predators, performance is better and that when such predators, be they animal, fungus or other pathogen, catch up with the crops or evolve to attack them, disaster follows, as occurred in the coffee harvests of Malaya at the beginning of the century and in the banana-growing countries of Central and northern South America before that. The corollary is seen where alien plants, contrary to expectation, appear to oust native plants in species-rich environments, where every 'niche' would appear to have been filled by species evolving more or less *in situ* to fit those environmental factors. Examples are *Hakea* (Proteaceae, Australia) and pines which have been able to take hold in the Cape. Exotics may appear to compete better with indigenous vegetation in Britain: possibly the success of sycamore can be seen in this way. The principle is, of course, the essence of biological control: the introduction of the predators or other pests of plants getting out of control may lead to their collapse in numbers. The most successful example is probably the reduction of American prickly pears (*Opuntia*, Cactaceae) in the rangelands of Australia by the introduction of the moth whose larvae feed on such cacti in the Americas.

The original hypothesis of Janzen, as made in connection with rain-forest trees, has been examined by Hubbell (10) who found that inter-tree distances observed in forests were smaller than the model would predict, in that if each tree species were packed into the forest at a density set by its adult nearest-neighbour distance, only a very small percentage of the observed species could coexist with it. This suggests that the micro-environmental argument may be important, and also disturbance or random factors. Furthermore, clumping is likely to be rather common in that the sheer numbers of seeds landing near the mother will in general mean that even if only a very small percentage of seeds or seedlings avoid predation, the odds are that the survivors will be near the mother tree.

6.2.3   *Combinations of factors*

A biotic effect may be attained via an environmental one as in the case of allelopathy favouring particular associations of plants, mentioned in Chapter 3. Furthermore, of those explanations that incorporate biotic and microenvironmental as well as disturbance effects, the most balanced account is that of Grubb (11), who used the term 'regeneration niche' to cover all the factors that affect a plant during its career from fertilized egg to death. According to this view, differences at any point in the natural history of the plants will allow their coexistence and an examination of related species' response to potential germination sites, shade-tolerance, pollination or dispersal mechanisms and so on will disclose these differences. These then are features of species or subdivisions of them, by geography or sex for example, leading to a consideration of the form of organisms, so that differences in morphological features may reflect different lifestyles in closely related species, which can coexist.

In the neotropical Lecythidaceae for example (12) all species have large circumscissile capsules, but such uniformity disguises a wide range of variation in the texture of the mesocarp, degree of dehiscence, and development of the aril into a fleshy or winged structure, with the result that different species are dispersed by birds, bats, monkeys, rodents, wind, water and possibly fish. Another example, the Brazil nut (*Bertholletia excelsa*) has an operculum or lid that opens inwards so that animals have to get the seeds out, while in *Gustavia* the mesocarp is brightly coloured so that, once damaged, it is attractive to animals. In others the seeds hang out on funicles and are dispersed by bats; others have persistent calyces which allow the fruit to float. Germination features may differ, as in species of *Shorea* (Diptocarpaceae) where, in Malaya, *S. curtisii* requires moister conditions than do *S. leprosula* or *S. parviflora*. It is also more tolerant of low light intensities following establishment and is thus able to regenerate under the shade cast by the palm, *Eugeissona tristis*. Clumps of particular species may reflect past tree-falls in this way. In Costa Rica, the size of clumps of *Cryosophila guagara* palms corresponded to the size of light gaps created by fallen trees (13).

However, a recent attempt to fit the flowering and fruiting features of 56 species of trees in the montane rain forest of Jamaica (14) disclosed slight interspecific temporal separation, but there was one common type of pollination (by insects) and one of dispersal mechanism (by birds), so that 'niche' separation in this sense is slight and the coexistence of the 56 species cannot be explained in this way.

Nevertheless, in ordinations of vegetation, the regeneration characteristics of assemblages of species may give meaning to the observed
distribution of vegetation types, rather than the terrestrial features of the
environment. This was revealed in Whitmore's classic study of the vegetation of Kolombangara in the relatively species-poor rain forest of the
Solomon Islands (15). The aim was to make a classification of the forest
types of the island using twelve selected large tree species when, as a
blessing in disguise, the forests were hit by a violent cyclone. The
regeneration strategy of each of the twelve species was worked out and the
percentage occurrence of certain of these differentiating the forest types on
the island reflected different meteorological regimes.

The element of disturbance is undoubtedly one which maintains diversity
and if this is removed, the species total may fall. Since 1923 on Barro
Colorado Island the numbers of species of reptiles, amphibians and birds
have fallen since the effect of the secondary habitats associated with
agriculture, prevalent there beforehand, has diminished. A similar effect is
seen in British woodlands where the maintenance of traditionally disturb-
ing management (like coppicing) keeps up species numbers of animals and
plants, whereas abandoning of such management leads to a decline.

In our attempt at understanding the diversity of tropical forests, using
the example of the trees, we have had to take into account all the features
of the plant which would appear to reflect the forces of natural selection in
terms of physical factors: meteorological, topographical, pedological, and
biotic ones. Added to this must be an element of chance in that not
everything can be evenly distributed nor is disturbance predictable, as
reflected in the 'first-come first-served' stands of pioneers. This is best
exemplified by islands, however, and by Krakatoa, with its suspended
succession, showing that with a chance introduction of some late successional species, diversity would probably increase. Again, an examination
of the isolated neotropical cloud-forests by Sugden (16), shows that under
certain conditions, the role of chance in terms of long-distance dispersal
may be as important as the environmental factors in promoting diversity.
The woody floras of those forests which are surrounded on all sides by arid
woodlands consist of species with wide neotropical distributions and
many of them are found elsewhere in a wide range of habitats while few
are restricted to montane forest. Many of them are pioneers, characteristic
of early successional sequences elsewhere, and are well adapted for
long-distance dispersal, so that under isolated circumstances such pioneers
can form 'mature' communities, even though the level of disturbance is
low.

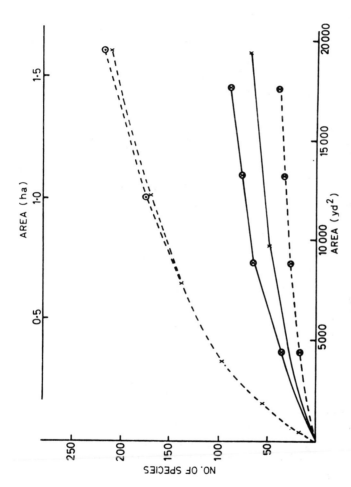

Figure 16 Species/area curves in tropical rain forest. Top to bottom: trees over 10 cm diameter at Bukit Lagong, Malaysia; the same at Sungei Menyala, Malaysia; the same in Guyana; trees over 28 cm diameter at Sungei Menyala; trees over 30 cm diameter in Guyana. Reproduced with permission from M. E. D. Poore in *Journal of Ecology* **52**, suppl. (1964) 221, Fig. 3.

In conclusion, it may be remarked that the greatest diversity is found where nutrient levels are low, but not too low, and where predation is high, but not too high. But as for an explanation of local heterogeneity, T. C. Whitmore at the end of his study of the Kolombangara forests, may be quoted. 'It can therefore be seen that variation from place to place in climax tropical lowland rain forest, which has for so long intrigued and challenged ecologists, is not open to any single or simple explanation. Rather, it is due to a complex interplay of extrinsic and intrinsic factors, which are not unique to the tropics and which have to be resolved individually for any particular forest'.

6.3 Practical problems

That there should be about 400 woody species in a hectare of South American or Malaysian forest has led to problems not only in accounting for such diversity, the main subject of this chapter, but also in actually measuring the richness of such forests. Sampling is likely never to be comprehensive in terms of the total number of species recorded from an area (see Fig. 16) unless almost the whole area is used as the sample. In a recent study 10 % of Barro Colorado Island was used in sampling and only 80 % of the known flora was found (4). The problem then arises that a sample of such size, or indeed any large plot, will mask any micro-topographical diversity in the forest and thus any local species assemblages under particular microenvironmental conditions.

In an attempt to reach a practical solution, Brünig and Klinge (17) worked in Amazonian forest which was estimated to have some 700 plant species, excluding cryptogams, representing 70 families. In view of the problem of the masking of environmental heterogeneity, they found that small plots of 40×50 m were the most profitable in terms of time and information gained (even though they recorded only 500 common tree species in 35 families), and that for phytomass studies small plots were adequate. Nevertheless, they stressed that any sampling design should be rigorously stratified according to site conditions and the stage of re-generation of the forest, and that measurements of parameters such as stand height, basal area and tree density in the areas around plots should also be taken. In this way, they argued, a reasonable picture of forest diversity and structure could be built up.

CHAPTER SEVEN

COEVOLUTION AND COEXISTENCE

In earlier chapters, it was noted that certain groups of animals came to prominence and greatly diversified as the angiosperms took over the domination of the land plant world: the insects, the mammals and the birds. At its simplest, the relationship between animals and plants, with the exception of insectivorous plants, which are not restricted to the tropics, is one of eater and edible, but it has also been noted that these particular groups have been implicated in the diversification, or the maintenance of diversity, of rain forest species of plant, while a little has been said of their distribution in forest, their seasonality and their changing prominence in pollination and dispersion during succession. In the last chapter, it was noted that some groups of trees employed in turn the same species of pollinating insects, suggesting that within certain constraints these were generalist in their flower-visiting. This contrasts with the often-repeated one-to-one association of certain orchids and their insects and of the hundreds of species of figs and theirs. How closely knit are animals and plants in rain forest?

7.1 Pollination

In the wet forests of Costa Rica (1) it was found that some 90 % of tree species were insect-pollinated, approximately the same percentage as in dry forest, so the insects will be considered first.

7.1.1 Insect-pollination (entomophily)

For insects, plants represent humid but well-drained surfaces and increase

91

the amount and diversity of living space (2), while for some, they represent food to browse, or a repository to bore into in egg-laying. Many different groups are involved in the pollination of angiosperms and, in rain forest (1), this seems to be rather bound up with the level in the forest at which the flowers are presented. In Costa Rica, the large and medium-sized trees were associated with generalist insects and not bats or birds, the almost exclusively tropical pollinators. Only 3 % of species there were visited by bats: a similar percentage was recorded for wind-pollinated trees. Hummingbirds and hawkmoths were largely associated with trees producing flowers near the forest floor, where noctuid moths were found to be important pollinators in the smaller species of Meliaceae and butterflies in such families as Rubiaceae. The scent-sensitive Lepidoptera were thus associated with the strongly-scented flowers in the relative calm there. Almost all the insects examined were generalists, particularly small bees that visited a wide range of the trees with rather small 'unspecialized' flowers. The stratification could be summarized as follows: large bees in the emergents, smaller bees in the lower reaches with other generalist insects, and near the forest floor everything, including wind, as pollinator.

In West Malaysia (3), there seems to be a clear distinction between the pollinators above and those below the canopy. Below, the flowers have minimal visual lures and are produced over extended periods, or even continuously, while others are strongly scented and produced more periodically. In the canopy, the flowers are larger and more conspicuous, as in almost all of the emergents. The pollinators in the lower regions are non-specific and include meliponid bees, solitary wasps and butterflies and also unspecialized beetles, midges, flies and thrips, all rather short-range pollinators. Most of these are also found in the upper canopy, although that is dominated by the wide-ranging bee, *Apis dorsata*, with *Xylocopa* bees also conspicuous. Sunbirds and bats, which live outside the forest, also work the flowers at this level. *Xylocopa* and the sunbirds were mostly found in the forest fringes, foraging on gap-phase plants though they moved to the mature forest trees during flowering periods. In the lower reaches of the forest, then, there is a constant but low level of presentation of a few flowers dealt with by low but more or less constant densities of animals, whereas in the upper layers, the flowers are more conspicuously advertised and draw such animals as birds, which are wider-ranging and with good sight, as well as the local, more stationary pollinators from lower in the forest.

The trees of the lower reaches are thus generalized in their attractions while trees like the dipterocarps get the local fauna and the bee *Apis dorsata*. Some trees such as Polygalaceae, two subfamilies of Leguminosae, *Papilionoideae* and *Caesalpinioideae*, have floral structures restricting access to the nectar or pollen to *Xylocopa* bees, a mechanism familiar enough in the temperate representatives of these families. Some of the dipterocarps, as was mentioned in the last chapter, are visited by thrips though these trees are strongly self-incompatible. Other ways in which outcrossing may result include the consequences of the aggressive behaviour of some of the pollinating bees, which may force other pollinators to withdraw from a particular tree and seek another. In mass-flowering, the thrips with their rapid breeding cycles and build-up of numbers may form a very high percentage of the pollinators. Possibly such mechanisms can be used to explain where the pollinators come from in species—poor forests such as the *Shorea albida* forest in Sarawak when the dominants flower.

Despite this apparent stratification, certain groups of plants are very restricted in their range of pollinators. Palms, which may vary in size from emergents in the montane forest of the Andes to treelets 30 cm tall in the Madagascan rain forest, are thought to be pollinated largely by beetles (2) and not, as was formerly believed, by wind. Indeed, many trees that look as though they might be adapted to wind-pollination are known to be pollinated by insects—like *Mallotus oppositifolius* (Euphorbiaceae) in West Africa, which has an attractive sweet scent—and it has been suspected that even forest-grasses are animal-pollinated.

Examination of particular species seems to show elaborate systems for enhancing cross-pollination. Many tree species are dioecious, although sometimes the rudiments of the opposite sex are found in the flowers. Such is the case in the majority of the Meliaceae, for example. The dioecious *Xerospermum noronhianum* ('*X. intermedium*', Sapindaceae) in West Malaysia (4) has a prolonged sequential development of flowers on each inflorescence as well as the sequential development of the inflorescences themselves, making a small number of flowers available at any one time but ensuring economy by not producing excess flowers within a short period (these would not be pollinated owing to the low density of pollinators). The major pollinators are short-distance generalists and the fidelity is maintained by the simultaneous flowering of trees of both sexes within close proximity. Furthermore, it was observed that female trees flowered less frequently: 22 % of the known females in the five-year study flowered more than twice, compared with 35 % of the males. This could be argued as promoting the crossing between different parent trees in successive seasons.

Insects collect pollen and, in the case of, for example, beetles, solid food bodies in or about the flowers. In a species of the palm genus, *Bactris*, the fleshy petals and sepals are eaten. Fleshy bracts of a species of *Freycinetia* (Pandanaceae) are eaten by rodents and birds, which are thought to pollinate it. Insects also collect nectar as a 'liquid reward' (5), a category that may include stigmatic secretions; these may be involved in insect nutrition as well as in pollen-tube germination. The extent of nectar production is apparently associated with pollinator size and there is variation in its sugar content and dilution. In dioecious species, the sugar proportions are different in male and female flowers. Apparently bat-pollinated flowers have hexose-dominated nectars, while sucrose predominates in hummingbird flowers and in those visited by some insects, but for bee-pollinated flowers as a whole, there is no obvious trend. The nectar also includes other constituents such as amino acids, present in low but important concentrations, highest in those nectars which are the only protein source for pollinators. Lipids are also found in the nectars of many plants but also in flowers of non-nectariferous species. The 'robbing' of nectar, familiar in temperate plants, is also prevalent in the tropics and bees may attack bird-pollinated flowers. Although it has been argued that nectar might contain repellents to ants which otherwise predominate on sugary substrates in the tropics, it is found that ants will take this nectar when it is presented to them, though the floral parts of such flowers may be less palatable (6).

7.1.2   Bird-pollination (*ornithophily*)

Bird-pollinators (7) include unspecialized nectar-eaters, which opportunistically visit many different kinds of flower, generally small ones, and specialized nectar-eaters, which concentrate on a few kinds of flower, mainly larger ones. Nectar never provides a complete diet for any of these birds, which also eat insects or other animals, but, as nectar is replenished as it is removed, birds may defend clumps of nectariferous flowers. In different continents, different groups of birds are nectarivorous—largely hummingbirds in the New World, sunbirds and sugarbirds in Africa and honey-eaters in Australasia. There is little overlap in the families of plants the different groups visit and, in those families, the flowers may look very different. For example, in Australasia the flowers are of an open type compared with the tubular form of the bird-pollinated flowers of South America and Africa. In short, it would seem that the relationship must have evolved over and over again. This is borne out by work on more temperate plants, for many of the hummingbird-pollinated plants of western North America belong to genera that are predominantly, and it is believed more anciently, insect-pollinated. It is often repeated that hummingbird flowers are red, part of the ornithophilous 'syndrome', and, indeed, red does seem to be preferred by these birds. Nevertheless, it may well be that such birds are conditioned to this colour and it has been shown that nectar quality can overcome colour prejudice. Again, it has been argued that colour contrast and other factors may be important for red contrasts well with green and many hummingbird plants with bluish leaves have yellow flowers, the complementary colour. Any amino acids in the nectar are probably of little importance and nectars high in them are avoided by the birds. The nectar is merely a high-energy source.

The unspecialized hummingbirds range over herbs to trees, which produce many flowers with little nectar which would attract pollinators. In a mass, however, the birds may defend the flowers and thereby reduce cross-pollination. The specialized hummingbirds do not normally maintain feeding territories or defend patches of flowers but 'trapline' to flowers on other plants of the same species. These plants are mainly large herbaceous ones or lianes or epiphytes, mostly different in form, then, from those attracting unspecialized hummingbirds.

In the more seasonal forests, hummingbirds may be migratory, but in all forests they tend to breed at the time when the flowers on which they depend are most abundant, though as with the thrips and the *Shorea* species, there is some staggering of flowering times and avoidance of competition for pollinators between plants. Bird nectar thieves like the flower-piercers are found in many species, but the bromeliads with thick protecting bracts are almost immune to their attacks. It has been argued (8) that the dilute nature of the nectar in such flowers deters some bee robbers which may be unable to concentrate it: the birds would prefer concentrated sugars. It has more frequently been suggested that dilute sources will promote visits to many flowers and thus out-crossing, though it is difficult to see how such a mechanism could arise, and perhaps it is more satisfactory to surmise that visits by a pollen-dusted vector to several flowers on one plant are promoted, leading to cross-fertilization of more. Nectar flow in the red-flowered *Brownea rosa-de-monte* (Leguminosae) of the Panama forests (9) is known to be influenced by interference from stingless bees and lepidopteran larvae, though, in general, flow in this species decreases through the day during which any flower is presented. Although the inflorescences last just one day, their production tends to be synchronized within localized groups of trees.

7.1.3   Bat-pollination (chiropterophily)

Of bats, which pollinate a small percentage of tropical rain forest trees, a minority feed exclusively on floral resources. Of these, in West Malaysia (10), two species roost singly in trees and fly short distances to feed upon trees which produce a few flowers all year round, and the third, *Eonycteris spelaea*, roosts in large colonies in caves and can fly up to at least 35 km from them to feed and take food from a wide range of flowers scattered in space and time. In Brazil, it was found by Hopkins (11) that in the genus *Parkia* (Leguminosae), five species flowered sequentially and were pollinated by the same bat species moving from one to the other in time. Concurrently, though, the destructive bruchid beetle populations which damage seeds moved from one fruiting species to another. It would therefore appear that the ensuring of successful pollination must override the importance of losses due to seed predation. Indeed, such compromises may be widespread.

Bat-pollinated plants, e.g. species of *Oroxylum* (Bignoniaceae) and *Duabanga* (Sonneratiaceae) in Borneo, are possibly most conspicuous along river banks where, incidentally, wind-pollinated trees such as species of *Octomeles* (Datiscaceae) and *Casuarina* (Casuarinaceae) are also found.

7.1.4   Other mammals

Non-flying mammals have for some time been suspected to be pollinators in a number of vegetation types outside the tropics and, in recent years, this has been proved to be so in both South Africa and Australia. It is now known that three species of forest plant in the Amazonian forest of south-east Peru (12) are visited by up to seven species of diurnal and six species of nocturnal non-flying mammals in the dry season. Heavy deposits of pollen were found on the facial fur of these animals. They might be considered likely to feed on flowers at a time, such as the dry season, when there is a scarcity of fruit. Of the species observed, the canopy liane, *Combretum fruticosum* (Combretaceae), was seen to be visited by primates including the pygmy marmoset, while the tree, *Quararibea cordata* (Bombacaceae), was visited by large primates, opossums and kinkajous. It was notable that in the Peruvian forest some four genera of marsupials were involved, members of the group which comprises all the non-flying mammalian pollinators of Australia.

7.2   Seed dispersal and predation

Compared with pollination, the process of dispersal is even more closely associated with the depleting of plant materials. Indeed, the line between 'predation' and dispersal-mechanism is hazy in that plants with a small numbers of seeds in any season may lose the whole crop to 'dispersal agents'. Rather than try to disentangle the scores of relationships examined between animals and plants in this area by putting them into categories of predation or dispersal mechanism, then, an attempt is made to look at the relationships of particular taxonomic groups of animals and their food plants.

Relative to other 'prey', fruits have evolved to be generally accessible, conspicuous and rather digestible when ripe (13). At one extreme, some plants produce many small, nutritionally poor fruits which attract a wide range of 'poor quality' dispersers, while at the other, some produce a smaller number of large, nutritionally superior fruits, dispersed by a limited number of species. Rarely, though, has it been demonstrated that only one species is associated with dispersal, in contrast to several examples known of one-to-one pollinator-pollinated relationships. On the contrary, the majority of studies of birds, for example, show that a wide range of species visits particular fruiting trees. Even the 'specialized' high-reward fruits of some Lauraceae may have the seeds dispersed by more than seventeen species of bird. Such birds may vary widely in morphology and taxonomic affinity. Most studies of this type have yet to evaluate the efficiency of such species as dispersers rather than visitors or feeders.

In pollination, the target for pollen is a stigma, which pollinators are encouraged by a number of lures and mechanical devices to brush, whereas the target sites for seeds are particular points suited to germination. In few cases does a dispersal agent deliver a seed directly to such a target other than by chance. Exceptions would be certain Loranthaceous seeds, which birds remove from their bills by brushing them through bark crevices, or the passage of seeds through an animal to germinate in its dung. Indeed, many seeds will not germinate unless they have undergone such passage or, at least, had the nutritious outer integument of the seed, an aril, removed. Again, the deposition of pollen is timed to suit its germination in that stigmas and anthers are synchronized, whereas the site for germination of a seed may occur randomly in time as well as space in the regenerating gaps of forest. A habitat specificity of a pollinator would improve pollination success, but it can be argued that in a dispersal agent this would lead to increased predation of seedlings, while it must be remembered that a site suited to germination of a particular tree species is no longer suited once an adult is in that place. Furthermore, pollinators are directed to suitable target sites for deposition of pollen by a series of rewards at those sites, whereas dispersers are not and indeed, jettisoning of the 'ballast' from their food as rapidly as possible is to their advantage.

A plant could in theory 'specialize' in a few generalist dispersers, just as a frugivore could specialize on a plant dispersed by many other species. In short, there is no theoretical reasoning for supposing that there should be mutual 'co-evolution' of dispersers and dispersed plants. On the contrary, a wide range of dispersal agents would allow a larger number of individuals to strip the tree of fruit at its prime and it would then be distributed to a wider range of habitats and be buffered against any disaster which might overcome the dispersal agent of a species relying on just one such agent. As far as the dispersers are concerned, being generalist would overcome the problems of poor years of any particular plant species, which in any case, rarely fruit continuously throughout the year. Furthermore, the common dispersal agents of tropical seeds are much larger than the pollination agents: few of them complete a life-cycle that would be compatible with the short flower-to-fruiting cycles of plants, more suited in this respect to close associations with insects, as in pollination. Not surprisingly, therefore, a number of large, principally frugivorous birds undergo marked seasonal movements during the year, in response to local variations in fruit abundance.

7.2.1   Birds

With these general views in mind, the relationship between different groups and their plants will be examined. Tropical bats and other mammals, particularly primates, and also lizards, may take fleshy fruits from trees, and other mammals and reptiles may disperse fallen fruits, but birds are most important overall. Mammal-fruits are often rather dull-coloured but highly scented, as opposed to the bright colours and relatively little scent of bird-dispersed fruits. Fleshy fruits of the type birds eat are often thought of as primitive in many features, that is to say that they share more characters with ancestral flowering plant fruits than do fruits with wind-dispersed seeds. This hypothesis (7) is supported by the fact that most plant families that produce bird-dispersed seeds are of very wide distribution and that several of them are held to be primitive, e.g. Annonaceae, Lauraceae, while several genera conspicuous in this trait are found in both tropical America and Australasia. Many of the families involved are represented in temperate countries by species with wind-dispersed fruits, e.g. the ashes, *Fraxinus*, in Oleaceae, many tropical species of which have drupes.

Although the families of plants involved are ancient, they are represented in tropical rain forest to different extents in different continents. In particular, the two most important families, Lauraceae and Palmae, are richly represented in the tropical Americas and Indomalesia including New Guinea, but poorly so in Africa. For example, the island of Singapore has more native species of palm than has the whole of the African continent. This probably explains why Africa is relatively rather poor in specialized frugivorous birds. The tropical American cotingas (Cotingidae) and manakins (Pipridae), and the birds of paradise of New Guinea, have no African counterparts. Because fruits have a limited range of presentation possibilities and in many respects mimic one another in attracting birds, the frugivorous avifauna is less diversified than the insectivorous. For example, in the New World the largely tropical groups, the cotingas and manakins, are together represented by only 140 species, whereas there are 370 species of flycatcher (Tyrannidae) and 220 species of antbird (Formicariidae). Again, the insectivores in closely related groups can coexist, whereas this is rare in the frugivores.

Birds range from the most unspecialized, which regularly take other foods besides fruits and cannot subsist on fruit alone, to the most specialized, absolutely reliant on the fruit. Of these, the unspecialized are typically opportunist, taking fruits as and when they become available. The fruits associated with such dispersers are conspicuous, produced in abundance, and are rathery watery, sugary and with little nutritive value, for they have little fat or protein. As with the plants visited by nectari-vorous birds, then, these plants provide a source of energy but not a whole diet. The fruits and seeds tend to be small. These are features of the early successional plants of clearings and forest edge, and, in Europe, would be exemplified by elder, *Sambucus nigra* (Caprifoliaceae), with its small shiny-black sweet fruits produced in abundance. By contrast, the most specialized frugivores are attracted in general to the large-seeded fruits, a common feature of later-successional species. In such plants, the seed is attractive in being covered with a layer of nutritious material. As it must be swallowed, the layer is not too thick, which may account for the common occurrence of relatively thin layers of nutritious material over a single seed or a few seeds in a fruit. Such a layer may be derived from carpellary structures, it may be an aril (a third integument of the seed), or a sarcotesta, which is a fleshy layer less readily removed, sometimes being an elaboration of one of the other integuments. Such fruits have high levels of protein and fat and are not very conspicuous. The specialized frugivore is typically a larger bird than the unspecialized one and may have a very wide gape, but also the capacity to strip the seed and regurgitate the ballast rather rapidly, while the fruit itself must be available all the year round. The specialized frugivores are, in general, foraging for only a short period of the day—in the cases of manakins and cotingas, for only some 10% of the daylight hours. (Such species also have social systems in which males spend almost all their time at display grounds while the females spend almost all of theirs performing nesting duties single-handed.)

In a moderately seasonal environment, in which a number of species produce fleshy fruits, there might be expected to be selection for a particular species to fruit out of step with the others, and thereby avoid competition with other species for dispersers. In *Miconia* (Melastomataceae) in an area of forest in Trinidad, as was explained in Chapter 6, a set of species with such staggered fruiting seasons produced available fruit all the year round between them.

In Panama (14), 60% of the seeds from the understorey tree, *Guarea glabra* (Meliaceae), were removed by four species of North American migrants, though there was no evidence that any single bird species was dependent on the tree for nutrition, nor the tree reliant on any one species of bird for dispersal. In the north temperate zone, the latitudinal range of fruiting season seems to be associated with the arrival of the southward-shifting, migratory, frugivorous birds such as thrushes. In the Mediterranean, where many such frugivores overwinter, bird-fruits tend not to ripen until winter, and show some of the attributes of tropical specialized fruits in that they are drier and more nutritious than northern fruits and can provide a complete diet for the birds. Notable then is the liane, ivy (*Hedera helix*, Araliaceae), the only member of its predominantly tropical family to reach northern Europe, for it produces unusually nutritious fruits which do not fully ripen until spring (it flowers in autumn) when these are fed to nestlings, whose diets are otherwise almost entirely of animal origin.

Another isolated tropical-type plant in northern Europe is the mistletoe, *Viscum album*, the only representative of Loranthaceae, a pantropical family. The relationship between the Loranthaceae and their birds—mistletoe birds (Dicaeeidae) of Indomalesia and Australasia, certain small neotropical tanagers and certain small African barbets—seems to be close. The birds are small like the fruits, and have short, rather stout bills, quite unlike the specialized frugivores discussed above. The seeds are embedded in a sticky material undigested by the bird's gut and are either voided through the gut, or, as in mistletoe, the sticky seed is scraped off in crevices in bark by the bird, which has first removed the fruit structures. A similar parallel is seen in the epiphytic cactus, *Rhipsalis*, the only cactus genus to be found outside the Americas, while birds may also be involved in the dispersal of the fruits of other epiphytes such as aroids and bromeliads.

Many birds eat seeds and are often referred to as seed-predators. Parrots and most pigeons, for example, are notorious seed-consumers. An argument for the co-evolution of dispersers and their trees is that they, in contrast, avoid the seeds, though in the past such seeds may have been in some way indigestible, promoting the relationship of today. Indeed, the seeds of such specialized plants as the Lauraceae of Trinidad are not, in general, attacked by parrots. Palms seem to have a mechanical defence in the form of a woody endocarp, familiar as the 'stone' of a date or the 'shell' of a coconut (not a bird-dispersed species!) As far as is known there is no toxic substance in palm fruits, but by contrast, the seeds of Lauraceae contain alkaloids: the avocado pear (*Persea americana*), for example, has a poisonous seed. Seed-predators which hoard seeds may be effective as dispersal agents: in temperate regions, nutcrackers and jays (Corvidae) store large numbers of seeds and exploit them later, and death or 'forgetfulness' of the bird will result in successful dispersal.

7.2.2 *Dispersal by several agents*

Most studies have been carried out by watching just one plant species and drawing conclusions from that, though a study by Leighton and Leighton (15) analysed a whole forest in eastern Borneo. Fruiting in general was found to be markedly seasonal, one dry period being followed by a massive flowering and fruiting. Predator satiation, particularly of primates and some squirrels, which seem to eat almost anything, was notably associated with some trees like many Euphorbiaceae. Of the predators, fruit pigeons were abundant on figs whose seeds are inviable thereafter, but they avoided, as in the Trinidad example, the large fruits, such as those of *Dysoxylum* (Meliaceae), which they would appear to be able to deal with (these fruits are dispersed by hornbills). Because of the seasonality of fruiting, the major question left unanswered is where the dispersal agents come from and where they go to. This has, of course, important implications for the appropriate sizes for nature reserves.

Of all large and medium-sized trees which fruit in the rainy season on Barro Colorado Island, 85% are animal dispersed and 12% wind-dispersed (16). Of those that fruit in the dry season, 36 % are animal-dispersed and 57 % wind-dispersed. Of smaller trees, almost 100 % of the wet-season fruiters are animal-dispersed as are only 35 % of the dry season ones, of which 21 % are wind-dispersed. In more seasonal regions, as in West Africa and South America compared with Indomalesia, for example, the percentage of wind-dispersed trees in the canopy is in general higher.

Some plants are known to be efficiently dispersed by two quite distinct types of agent. The pioneer *Cecropia glazioui* (Moraceae), of the coastal rain forest of south-east Brazil (17), is visited by three tanager species by day and three species of fruit bat by night, all in search of fruit. The minute hard fruits are ingested with the fleshy perianth and later dispersed through defaecation, though only 32 % of those passed through birds would germinate compared with 78 % from the bats. Fruit bats in Malesia press small-seeded fruits against their palates and drop the dried dross including the seeds. In this way figs, *Muntingia calabura* (Tiliaceae, introduced from the West Indies, but fruiting all year round) and species of *Melastoma* are dispersed. The exotic *Piper aduncum* from South America has probably recently been spread around Kuala Lumpur, Malaysia, in this way. Of species dispersed by birds and primates, the latter may sometimes surpass the birds in spreading seeds. For instance, in *Stemmadenia donnell-smithii* (Apocynaceae), spider-monkeys may excel over parrots and other birds in this respect (18) in Guatemala.

In a study of the Panamanian rain forest tree, *Tetragastris panamensis* (Burseraceae), visited by a wide range of animals, it was found that three mammal species accounted for over 97 % of the seeds removed from the tree (19), the howler monkey (*Allouatta palliata*) alone being responsible for 74 %. A number of other mammals and birds probably also disperse a very small proportion of the seeds, while two parrot species are the important seed-predators among a number of mammals and birds which destroy seeds. From 19 study trees in one season, fewer than 4 % of the total of more than 430 000 seeds produced had a chance of establishing, for 6 % were killed by the parrots, 66 % fell under the mother trees and 24 % germinated in close competitive clumps in faeces. Even lower percentages are estimated for *Shorea ovalis* (Dipterocarpaceae) in Malesia, where there was 83 % abortion, possibly due to the failure of pollination, while 90 % of the survivors were killed by a single insect predator species before being dropped. Sixteen per cent of the survivors on the ground were then killed by three other insect species and although mortality declined with distance from the mother tree, it was not due to host-specific predation (20). In a study of a forest as a whole, the Budongo Forest in Uganda, it was found that 40 % of all seeds were eaten by rodents before and immediately after germination and about a further 30 % were killed in two years by browsing antelope, while there were further losses from seed rot, insect and fungal attack and drought. The result was some 2 % survival of the seeds as saplings in two years.

Compared with most of the species mentioned so far, many figs seem to produce fruits almost all year round and are the most important foods of many specialized frugivores in Africa, Malesia and Australasia—the siamang (*Hylobates syndactylus*) in Malaya spends a quarter of its feeding time in fig trees. In the New World, bird species are less restricted to fig species (21), even if fruit is available continuously, as was found for individuals of two *Ficus* species in Panama which between them produced fruit all year round (22). In both these species, though, the major fruiting peak occurred when most other species were not in fruit, and it is suggested that the two species fruit asynchronously at relatively short intervals. This would seem to be linked with the capacity to provide egg-laying sites all the year round for the obligate fig-wasp pollinators, as well as to the year-round provision of food for the specialized dispersal agents such as howler monkeys and bats.

7.2.3   Some primates

Howler monkeys in Veracruz, Mexico spend an equal proportion of their time eating leaves and eating fruits (23) and concentrate on some 36 plant species, predominantly Lauraceae, Leguminosae and Moraceae. They eat up to 100 % leaves at some times of the year, but they seem efficient as seed dispersers, for some 60 % of seeds (seed sample of 8000) retrieved from their faeces germinated.

Although the orang-utan of Sumatra and Borneo (24) is primarily a fruit-eater, it takes a wide variety of foods including leaves, young shoots, flowers, pith and bark and occasionally mineral-rich soil, insects and possibly small vertebrates and birds' eggs. Plants in some 34 families were used in Borneo over a period of 16 months and all but five were sources of fruit. The apes fed on a wide range of foods at all times of the year, but when fruit was scarce, they spent more time travelling and turned to less nutritious plant materials as well. Of the 28 chief fruit species taken, 18 were rare (fewer than two trees per hectare), six occasional (two to four per hectare) and four had four to eight per hectare. Individuals of a few species like durians provide food for several orang-utan meals, but most are cleared by one animal in a single meal. In rainy weather, they sometimes concentrate on the less nutritious foods rather than search for more fruit, but in fruiting trees seem not to pay much attention to other frugivores though they eat most and that wastefully. Because of the scattered distribution of food, the orang-utan population is split up into small dispersed foraging units and the flexible nature of orang-utan society allows them to exploit irregular fruit distribution better than do territorial monkeys or gibbons, for example. The monkeys live largely on leafy shoots and eat fruit when it is available, while the gibbons have become largely specialized for diets of figs. Furthermore, the orang-utan can tolerate a wide range of bitter and sour fruits and high alcohol levels and its strong hands allow it to open spiny or hard fruits like durians and legumes.

The Sumatran orang-utan seems to be an important dispersal agent for some *Aglaia* spp. (Meliaceae) but durian seeds are so damaged that ground-walking animals are thought to be the principal effective agents— possibly sun-bears, or even tigers. Man has also been suggested—it has also been pointed out that the fruits favoured by him and the ape are the same. Possibly, then, the orang-utan has been excluded from the ground through competition with man, and has become arboreal, perhaps also as a result of being hunted for 30 000 years by his competitor.

7.2.4 *'Anachronisms'*

Although parrots have been treated as seed-predators, they are not always so, for they appear to be the principal dispersal agents of seeds of several species of *Parkia* (Leguminosae) in the Neotropics (25), as well as certain Lecythidaceae there, even though they are partly destructive. It may well be that the gum which surrounds the seeds of these species of *Parkia* and not of the seeds of the Palaeotropical ones is important here. Some other *Parkia* species are dispersed by agoutis and it is possible that others may have been adapted to dispersal by large terrestrial herbivores that are now extinct. About 10 000 years ago (26), over fifteen genera of Central American large herbivores became extinct so that the megafauna, previously comparable with that of Africa before the decimations caused by man, largely disappeared. Those that became extinct included gomphotheres (mastodon-like proboscidians), ground sloths and equids. The plants that these animals dispersed may thus be seen as vegetable anachronisms and the introduction of horses and cattle in historical times seems to have locally restored the ranges of such trees as jicaro (*Crescentia alata*,

Bignoniaceae) and guanacaste (*Enterolobium cyclocarpum*, Leguminosae) which may fall in this category.

Such anachronisms are likely to be common in those regions from which the large forest animals have been lately removed and may, in any case, be a common feature in evolution (27). Some of the woody lobelioids of Hawaii have thorns and toxins, apparently noxious to the type of herbivores not found in these islands, but possibly on the mainland where their ancestors came from (28). Another example of a dispersal anachronism is the extraordinary palm, *Lodoicea maldivica*, now restricted to small areas of the Seychelles. This tree is familiar to botanists because it has the largest seed known, as well as one of the largest leaves. The leaves of palms in general are often used for thatching and are relatively durable compared with most tropical foliage. The leaf litter of this remarkable plant is therefore bulky and relatively persistent. A single fallen leaf can smother a wide area of seedlings and it is perhaps no surprise then to learn that it has such a large seed which could not only penetrate this mass but have enough stores to supply a seedling as it grew up through it. Nevertheless, these large seeds are rather unlikely to be moved uphill by dispersal agents, particularly as there are no large animals on the island where the palm grows. It seems then (possibly retarded by a cotyledonary stalk up to 3 m long), to be slowly moving downhill as a species. The seeds are not resistant to salt water and immersion kills them. In short, this species is 'adapted' to going extinct. How did it reach the Seychelles? A clue may be found in the geology of those islands, for some of them are granitic and part of the Gondwanaland which linked India and Africa when they were adjacent. Is it then a relic of the greatest antiquity (29)?

7.2.5 Fish and ants

Dispersal agents not mentioned so far include fish. Some seeds of rheophytic plants are fish-dispersed and fish dispersal gets round the perennial problem of how plants can move 'upstream'. One such rheophyte is *Dysoxylum angustifolium* in the Pahang River basin in West Malaysia. In the same family (Meliaceae), in the allied genus *Guarea* in South America, *G. guidonia* is fish-dispersed. This mechanism seems to have arisen in parallel in these plants. Growing in the same river as *D. angustifolium*, but in other places as well, is another rheophyte in the same family, *Aglaia scortechinii*, which may also be fish-dispersed. In the case of the *Dysoxylum*, the fish flesh is rendered rather unpalatable by substances from the seeds. The indigenous people avoid these fish during the tree's fruiting season and, if other fish predators do the same, the tree could be said to be operating a Securicor system for its offspring. In the peat-swamp forest of Sarawak, the commercially important *Gonystylus bancanus* (Thymelaeaceae) is distributed by a small catfish, the strange flavour of whose flesh at different times of the year is attributed to the tree's arils. In the inundated *várzea* forest of the Amazon, sixteen out of thirty-three species examined had their seeds distributed by fish. In these nutrient poor waters, the fishes may be reliant on such vegetable input (30) and, in turn, the homogeneity of the inundated forests of Amazonia may be related to this fishy connection.

Invertebrates are less conspicuously involved in seed dispersal, but there are many examples of ant-dispersed seeds in temperate countries, e.g. species of *Carex* (Cyperaceae), *Ulex* (Leguminosae), and *Viola*, whose seeds are attractive because of oil-bodies, often rudimentary arils. A recently reported tropical example (31) is of two arrowroot relations, *Calathea* spp. (Marantaceae) in the Mexican rain forests. Of the twenty-one species of ant attracted to the arillate seeds, there are predatory *carnivorous* ponerines, which bear off the seeds, like animal prey, to the nest, where the nutritious arils are removed. The aril-less seeds have higher rates of germination than the undivested ones and the distribution of seedlings matches the ants' behaviour patterns.

7.2.6 *Specificity*

Where there is great specificity in seed-dispersal, a state of affairs which seems in general very rare, the disappearance of the dispersal agent is the road to extinction for the plant. Only elephants can swallow the pyrene of *Panda oleosa* (Pandaceae) and collected seeds do not germinate unless passed through an elephant, in whose dung they germinate. The seed content of droppings throughout one year in a rain forest in Ivory Coast (32) comprised some thirty-seven species of trees and five of herbs. Of the trees, only seven are known to be dispersed by monkeys or birds as well. Some 30 % of the trees whose dispersal agent is known in these forests are dispersed by elephants. It may well be that other such cases as the *Panda* represent extreme forms of the 'anachronisms' and that, formerly reliant on a number of dispersal agents, only one of these is now left. A celebrated example is that of a species of *Calvaria* (Sapotaceae), only geriatric trees of which could be found in Mauritius, to which island it is restricted. An inspired guess was made that the failure of the seeds to germinate was because its seeds had not passed through the gut of the dodo (*Raphus cucullatus*), extinct since 1681. This led to forced feedings of turkeys, and, after being voided, resultant germination of seeds of the tree which was on the verge of extinction.

7.3 Herbivory

In the last chapter, the role of grazing insects was examined. Some of the earliest known fossil vascular plants, those of the Rhynie Chert of the Devonian (2) 370 m years ago, show damage, which might be attributable to biting arthropods. Cockroaches and dragonflies appeared in the Upper Carboniferous (300 m years ago), at the same time as the giant clubmosses, ferns and seed-ferns; beetles are known from the Permian, and flies and wasps from the end of the Jurassic and Early Cretaceous when the angiosperms were diverging from their seed-fern ancestors. Today, herbivory in the crowns of mature trees in lowland rain forest in geographically distinct regions in the New and Old Worlds leads to 13.8–14.6 % tissue loss (33) in the leafy branches of trees, but consistently less in epiphytes, while in Ghana it has been shown that those plants with a rapid flush of leaves are consistently less severely attacked than those with a slower leaf production (34). There are many examples of increased attack of seedlings associated with closeness to the mother tree. This is not an exclusively tropical phenomenon: seedlings of Chinese Elm, *Ulmus parvifolia*, under the canopy of the mother tree at Albuquerque, New Mexico, were found to suffer some 580 times as much attack from the elm leaf beetle, *Pyrrhalta luteola*, as those beyond it (35).

Some of the most spectacular herbivory, besides the outbreaks of caterpillars in dipterocarps mentioned in Chapter 4, are the activities of leaf-cutting ants. *Atta cephalotes* builds nests up to 150 m^2 in surface area, containing several million workers. These may persist for up to 20 years (36) and such a nest in rain forest can completely defoliate a major tree in a single night. It takes some five or six years for a nest to produce sexual insects, so that it would appear that the complete defoliation of the immediate area or the removal of the more palatable species would lead to deteriorating conditions for the ants. In other words, in the long term, the maximum energy return for a given energy output in the short term would seem inappropriate. Evidence suggests that, on the contrary, grazing pressure is evenly spread throughout the area exploited, that area is related in size to the size of the nest and that it is defended against competing leaf-cutting ants and that a wide range of plant species is exploited. When the forest is felled, however, and replaced by monocultures of, for example, fruit trees, with a much reduced number of leaves per hectare, the system breaks down and there is often widespread crop damage.

Ants are not always involved in such an apparently one-sided relationship with plants, as we have seen in the case of myrmecophytes. In Central America, they are associated with *Acacia* trees, which, if purged of their ants, are grazed out or become covered with lianes (37) which the ants discourage. Ants are found in the young shoots and petioles of many plants, though this is not always the case in all individuals of particular species, e.g. *Chisocheton* (Meliaceae) or *Macaranga* (Euphorbiaceae). In *Barteria nigritana* (Passifloraceae) in Africa one coastal subspecies is inhabited by one species of ant, but the more widespread other subspecies has another ant species, though again not all specimens are infected. Although ants may prevent other insects raiding the plant's resources, they may also tend mealy bugs which are a drain on the plant (38). Although no apparently obligate ant-plant symbiosis is found north of latitude 24°N, ants are also involved in seed dispersal in temperate species, as we have seen.

The weighing up of 'advantage' and 'disadvantage' here and in general is extremely difficult and will change with time and locality. Furthermore, defences—mechanical or chemical properties such as tannins which make digestion hard (though the effect greatly varies in magnitude) or toxins such as alkaloids—are no deterrent to some animals. There may be variations in toxin levels with the season, and animals, in any case, eat different parts of plants with different levels of toxin and, at different stages of their own development, may be able to deal differently with such toxins (39). It has even been suggested (24) that alkaloid level fluctuations may affect the feeding patterns of orang-utans through the day. Black colobus monkeys (*Colobus satanas*) in the coastal rain forest of Cameroon (40), avoid young and mature leaves of most of the common plants in their habitat and feed disproportionately heavily on the leaves of rare plants. The preferred foods are rich in mineral nutrients and in nitrogen, and low in the digestion-inhibitors, tannin and lignin. They differ from other colobines in eating seeds, which they may be able to detoxify in the fore-stomach.

The relationship between herbivores and plants has often been seen as some kind of arms race, but there have been opposing views in that, for example, spittle-bugs in the dry tropics of West Africa, rather than depleting valuable water resources may promote microbial activity beneath particular tree species, allowing them to take up nutrients in the dry season from the surface layers of the soil, provided that other roots can tap a deep water source. Such are the 'raining trees' of Africa (41). This attractive hypothesis has been extended to other groups of plants and their 'consumers' suggesting that under certain circumstances plants may benefit from those animals that feed on them and, indeed, may positively 'encourage' such herbivory. The step from predation to this symbiosis is a short one.

One such hypothesis with respect to tropical trees argues that the solid bole of a tree locks up an enormous amount of nutrients and that, if this could be recycled by 'employing' micro-organisms to rot down the heartwood, thus providing a roost for animals whose nests and droppings would subsequently rot too, the roots of long-lived organisms like trees would be prevented from exhausting local resources and competing with other roots, and the chemicals produced to prevent heartrotting would be saved. The discovery of a species of *Guarea* (Meliaceae) with its own roots growing up into its hollow trunk, shortcircuiting the nutrient cycle, seemed excellent evidence in support of the hypothesis (42), though in Jamaica it was found that many such hollow trees were full of roots, but some of them were from trees not merely of different individuals, but of different species!

A final example from the zoological side should suffice to show why ecology does not lend itself to the clearcut generalization as investigations of interactions are intensified. The relationship between ants and their aphids, farmed to produce honeydew from plant hosts, is complicated in itself but, in the Old World Tropics, mosquitoes of the genus *Malaya* are associated in their habits with certain ants which run up and down tree-trunks carrying the honey-dew they have taken from their aphids. The mosquito (43) hovers a couple of centimetres from the trunk and suddenly alights in front of the ant. It does not touch it but vibrates its wings: in response the ant opens its jaws, between which the mosquito pushes its proboscis and filches the honey dew. And what eats the mosquito?

CHAPTER EIGHT

RAIN-FOREST MAN

Most fossil evidence of early man comes from East Africa and, until recently, Africa has been almost unchallenged as the place of divergence of man's immediate ancestors from other hominids. New evidence from the Middle East (1) suggests that it may not be so simply explained, while a recently published account of a biologist's view of the myths embedded in Genesis lends some colourful support to a broadening of outlook (2). The thesis of that view is that man originated in rain forest and not in the more open habitats associated with the African finds. Generally, however, man is thought to have been living in the Malesian region and in tropical America at dates variously estimated between 25 000 and 40 000 years ago, and in Australia by 32 000 years ago. All these groups seem to have been nomadic or partly so. In Malesia, they seem to have made use of the limestone caves for shelter and may well have forced the orang-utans of the region to live further up in the canopy, for it is certainly true that in the Pleistocene, the orang-utans were much more terrestrial in habit (3).

The forest does not offer the grazing typical of animal husbandry and neither the plants nor the animals of domestication are forest organisms (4). Pre-agricultural man as a forest-dweller would have left no trace, though it has been entertainingly argued by Corner that traces of forest-life are embedded in modern society: he considers that the range of form in Pacific war clubs shows a gradation from the wrenched-up sapling, with its roots as spikes, to the mace of regalia. The digging stick of the forest becomes a spade, still with a wooden handle; lianes lead to ropes and string, bark and palm fibre to textiles, palm leaves to thatching and bamboos to piping. But the trick of firing the forest and thus a mechanism for massive clearing, is associated with seasonal forest, where man must have first made his mark.

It is difficult to assess the effects of the first men in rain forests, but it has been argued that the Australian aborigines may have been responsible for the removal of some of the *Araucaria* forest of tropical Queensland, leading to the advance of *Eucalyptus* there, as well as locally exterminating much of the megafauna. Truly forest people still survive in the dwindling rain forests of the three tropical masses: the Amazon Indians, the pygmies of the western part of Central Africa, and groups in the Andaman Islands, parts of West Malaysia and Borneo as well as the Philippines. Forest people are generally small and hence have a low maximal work capacity. They suffer from many parasitic diseases, and have high levels of infant and child mortality. An example of forest knowledge is that of the hunter gatherers on the Philippine island of Mindanao, who recognize 1600 categories of plants. Although the Andaman Islanders still do not know how to start fire from scratch, wholesale clearing of other parts of the tropics has long been practised. Drainage ditches some 9000 years old have been claimed for the highlands of New Guinea, a region under intensive clearing for some 5000 years, while pollen records indicate forest clearance a thousand or possibly three thousand years ago at Lake Victoria in Central Africa. It must be remembered, though, that the majority of modern African forest dwellers are secondary invaders with knowledge of agriculture and iron tools, and may have been there only some 2000 years (5).

Maize and beans have been cultivated in Central America for 7000 years and the form of farming known as shifting cultivation has gone hand-in-hand with the clearances in New Guinea over the last 5000 years. As with the clearance of the forest of the British Isles since the last glaciation, those areas with the 'least resistance', i.e. with shallow dry soils, have been cleared first. In such places regeneration is slowest, as can be seen from those areas of dry monsoon forest, long cleared away in East Java or around Angkor in Kampuchea. In time, plants were domesticated and selected so that they differ greatly from their wild ancestors, some so much so that their ancestors cannot now be recognized. In Asia, such 'cultigens' include the coconut, which may have had its origin on the Great Barrier Reef, and the mango and the betel nut, a palm (*Areca catechu*) with narcotic fruits. Plants now known only in cultivation but whose ancestry is fairly clear include sugar-cane and rice and bananas which are sterile triploids, many of those involving hybridity between a rain forest species, *Musa acuminata* and *M. balbisiana* of drier forests.

Purseglove (6) has argued that Indian crops were known in China 4000 years ago and African ones in India, and *vice versa*, a thousand years later. In the New World, there was movement of crops between Mexico and coastal Peru by 1000 B.C. and, a few hundred years later, the people of southern Arabia were trading down the coast of East Africa. Important commodities were spices, the control of which was largely responsible for European involvement and exploration leading to the Spanish and Portuguese colonizations and ultimately to the Dutch monopoly of nutmegs and cloves in Indonesia by the end of the eighteenth century. Contact with mariners from China from before A.D. 300 led to trade in a number of commodities in the Asiatic tropics, notably resins, birds' nests, poisons, medicines, latex, pelts, ivory and rhinoceros horn as well as rattans. All are still traded today, the rattans being the stems of climbing palms largely used in 'cane' furniture-making and sometimes referred to erroneously as bamboo. By A.D. 500, there were probably bananas in Madagascar, imported from Asia, though some authorities believe Madagascar was not in effect colonized by man until 500 years after that. By A.D. 700, there were coastal settlements in East Africa, made by the Arabs on slaving enterprises into the interior, and, along their routes, the mango, initially from India, became naturalized.

The original forest peoples of the tropics have been greatly reduced, or at least the territory through which they could formerly move has. The Amerindians have been in retreat since European invasion some 500 years ago, and a number of groups of them have been intensively studied. It is thought that they moved into the Amazon basin some 10 000 years ago (7) and that there are some generalized cultural patterns which can be recognized. They have extended families of a man, his wife or wives, preadolescent children and married sons (patrilocal residence) or daughters (matrilocal), and their children, in a communal house. A group of such households makes up a village and between such groups there is usually hostility from simple avoidance of one another to open warfare. At puberty, males become warriors and killing an enemy is often a prerequisite of attaining full adult status. Women and children may be captured from other groups and incorporated.

It is instructive to compare the ways the forest is exploited by two groupings of Amerindians far apart on the *terra firme* of Amazonia, the Jívaro, in the west under the slopes of the Andes, and the Kayapó in the east. The Jívaro occupy some 65 000 km² in the eastern lowlands of Ecuador and comprise some 20 000 people, women outnumbering men by about two to one. In spite of common language and culture, there is no permanent social or political cohesion. In fact, blood revenge and warfare are more intense between the constituent subgroupings than they are between them and other groups. Each village consists of a single house of a patrilineal extended family with 15–46 members. The house is abandoned when hunting is unproductive, the local fields are exhausted or the head of the village dies, so that in general one site is used for about six years. The Jívaro depend largely on agriculture and do not eat many wild plants, though they hunt a lot. Inter-village hostility may include the abduction of women or the murder of a member passing through alien territory, while a series of deaths in a village may be interpreted as the result of sorcery on the part of other villages. Such events require that the adult males take blood revenge and a single death restores the balance. Total warfare, though, aims at the annihilation of the enemy village, the death of all its inhabitants, the burning of the house and its contents and even the uprooting of the crops. It is plain, then, why men are in the minority. Sorcery and warfare lead to a thinly distributed, but quite large, mobile population. If the population declines, then so does the level of revenge killings and warfare. The population is also regulated by periodic suspension of sexual relationships for three to six months after the taking of a head and also from the time of birth of a child until he is weaned, i.e. two to three years. Each man has two or more wives and because adultery on the part of females carries the death sentence, the birth rate is rigorously controlled. As the whole system is headed by a man, it is likely that the village has to move more frequently than if it were headed by a woman. What seems barbarous is admirably suited to the rain forest environment, for the scattering of the groups, their rigorous population control and their constant movement mean that the forest is nowhere completely depleted and recovers through cycles of regeneration before being farmed once more. The system represents a remarkable evolutionary adaptation of human behaviour patterns to the conditions of the rain forest.

The Kayapó of Pará, Brazil, unlike the Jívaro, live in a seasonal climate with a marked dry spell each year. The general pattern is the same in that the village is the largest political unit and that the cultural and linguistic inter-village similarities do not prevent hostility. In this group, the extended family may include some hundreds of people, while the time of greatest status for a male is that between puberty and parenthood. This has led to the adoption of a wide range of contraceptive techniques including the use of oral contraceptives (the biological origins of which are now eagerly sought by pharmaceutical companies). They also practise mechanical forms of abortion. Monogamy is universal but adultery frequent. The group subsists on gardening and hunting. The full status for the male is achieved only after killing an enemy, who, by definition, is anyone not a member of the home village. In this group, though, not every man need kill, for a blow dealt to the body during a war is sufficient. In major assaults, the village is burnt and the women and children captured and incorporated in the community. The Kayapó population density is twenty times that of the Jívaro and the villages are maintained indefinitely in one place only, at the cost of a periodic temporary increase in community mobility. In the dry season, groups of families travel out into the forest, moving camp every few days and living off wild foods, thus more uniformly exploiting the environment at a time of scarcity and the risk of irreversible depletion of the local forest. Parallels between these two patterns of human behaviour and those of pioneer trees on the one hand or leaf-cutting ants on the other are clear.

The forest peoples of the Malay Peninsula, the *orang asli*, include one nomadic group, the Negritos—who may have been the first to arrive in the Peninsula, some 25 000 years ago (8)—while other groups are permanently settled, and the rest practise some form of shifting (swidden) cultivation. The Temiar, for example, will stay up to fifteen years in one settlement until travelling to more and more distant areas of cultivation becomes too troublesome, when they will move. Although there is a Temiar area over which this is carried out, there is no personal land tenure, though particular fruit trees may have owners. Such is the case with durians, which may be inherited. When a new site is chosen for cultivation, the undergrowth is removed, and later the trees, with an adze. The stumps and roots are left as are many big trees for superstitious or practical reasons (the two may be the same in many cases). Such a tree is the *tualang* (Fig. 10), *Koompassia excelsa*, which has hard useless timber but harbours bees' nests. Also left are useful fruit trees, which are thus under selective pressures. The dead material is left to dry, is then burnt and left to cool; planting in the fertilizing ash takes place after the first rain. The protein part of the diet is supplemented by hunting using bamboo blowpipes with the nerve poison strychnine, an alkaloid from species of *Strychnos* or from *Antiaris toxicaria*, the upas tree (Moraceae), or venom from toadskin or snakes. Trapping and fishing are also important. The gardens consist of a wide range of plants, apparently growing haphazardly and far from the regimented uniformity of plantation agriculture.

Certain groups of tropical peoples grow an enormous range of plant species. An outstanding example (9) is provided by the Lua of northern

Thailand who grow at least 120 different crops: 75 for food, 21 for medicine, 20 for ceremony and decoration and 7 for weaving and dyeing, a diversity which mimics the diversity of natural vegetation. The breadth of the food base is also seen in settled communities in the Malay Peninsula, where villagers may collect some wild fruit species but grow many in and around the village. Whitmore (3) recorded 29 types of tree around such a village in Trengganu, noting that twelve of them were identical with wild forest trees, such as the *rambutan* (*Nephelium lappaceum*, Sapindaceae) and the *sentul* (*Sandoricum koetjape*, Meliaceae), a further six appeared to be selected and improved forms of wild trees, five were cultigens like the betel nut, and three were exotics, like the papaya (*Carica papaya*, a New World cultigen).

When the cultivators move on, they leave a tangle of exotic and native plants including fruit trees, which they have deliberately planted or encouraged, and may scatter seed of useful plants before leaving. In New Guinea, such include *Artocarpus* (Moraceae), *Terminalia* (Combretaceae) and *Inocarpus* (Leguminosae). There, *Pandanus* trees are also planted in gullies and bogs. The effect of the distribution of such plants and in consequence the status of the regenerating forest was noted in Chapter 1. The history of the domestication of many of the fruit trees of the tropics may therefore never be disentangled, though it is known that some of them at least, like the *duku* and *lanseh*, forms of *Lansium domesticum* (Meliaceae), are apomicts.

It is not only the botanist who is troubled by the culture of tropical civilizations before the intrusion of western man. Remarkable disjunctions in the distributions of neotropical birds have been explained by their deliberate introduction to new areas by pre-Columbian bird-fanciers. Thus Haemig (10) has argued that between 1486 and 1502, the great-tailed grackle (*Quiscalus mexicanus*) was introduced from its original home in Veracruz to the Valley of Mexico by the Aztec Emperor, Auitzotl. Similarly, the painted jay, *Cyanocorax dickeyi*, in western Mexico is found some 4000 km from the possibly conspecific white-tailed jay, *C. mystacalis* of Ecuador and Peru, and may thus be another pre-Columbian exotic introduction. Again, tiger teeth found in Bornean caves are believed to have been placed there by man and not to indicate the former presence of the animal on that island (3).

CHAPTER NINE

THE CHANGING FOREST TODAY

We have already observed, that the most luxurious vegetation of spontaneous growth affords us certain proof that the soil which has produced it will prove equally favourable for the production of the usual objects of culture (George Finlayson, *Mission to Siam and Hué . . . in the years 1821–2*, (1826) p. 57).

9.1 Forest conversion

9.1.1 *Farming and gardening*

The slash-and-burn type of shifting cultivation has been used continuously for some 2000 years in Indomalesia, each patch being cropped for only two or three years, the people at a density of some five or fewer cultivators per square kilometre. It is a practical and successful way of utilizing land used throughout the tropics under different names, where poor soils, steep slopes and heavy rainfall obtain (1). It is successful where temperate zone type methods are not, and is generally held to be the most efficient in terms of soil recovery. Formerly considered the bane of tropical forests, it is now praised, possibly too much so, as a result of the increasing romanticization of forest-living, for shifting cultivation is changing. With the arrival of western man, who took spices and introduced new crops, has come plantation agriculture and a reduction in the mortality rate. Smallholder agriculture has led to the concentration of people being three times that which would support shifting cultivation in some areas. There is insufficient

116

time for the land to recover between cultivations and, largely through the agency of western man, exotic weeds have become established and encroach on the smallholdings. Inevitably, more forest land is brought under cultivation to counter this.

Before man started burning the forest, fires were the result of lightning, which is more common in the tropics than out of it, and possibly of falling rocks and, in wooded savanna, fermentation under compaction. In New Guinea, in the seasonal forests of the Gogol Valley, is evidence of major fires, for *Intsia* spp. (Leguminosae), which readily regenerate after fire, make up some 25% of the log volume there. In Africa, it is argued that man was using fire some 50–55 000 years ago, taking coals from camp to camp and using the fire to smoke out bees from their nests in honey-hunting, or driving game. This probably also occurred in the drier types of forest and savanna. Nevertheless, tropical rain forest may be flammable at the edges, so that savanna may spread. It has been calculated that because of burning only some 60% of Africa potentially covered with forest actually bears it today. The effects of fire are to increase light intensity at the ground, affecting germination but also the fauna and flora of the soil. There is an increase in evaporation and rain has more impact. Nitrogen is rapidly lost but immediately available potassium, magnesium and calcium increase as input from the ash. Run-off is increased, especially on slopes, and there may be marked compaction or other deterioration of the soil structure. Burnt sites improve grazing and tend to concentrate herbivores such as elephant and buffalo or antelope, some of which, in turn, attract concentrations of carnivores.

After burning in the Indomalesian region, grasses appear and, if these are left without grazing or burning, will slowly be replaced by the forest. If there is grazing or cutting, the grass composition may change and, if burnt, leads to the domination by *lalang* (*Imperata cylindrica*) a grass which is very difficult to eradicate. Continuous use of the land for cropping leads to declining yields, such that rice production, for example, may be halved in three years, partly due to nutrient removal, erosion, the physical deterioration of the soil and partly to the multiplication of pests and diseases and an increase in competition from weeds. Relic terraces and raised fields in the Mayan lowlands of Central America have been interpreted as indicative of a settled, sophisticated, intensive, prehistoric agriculture, rather than shifting cultivation, which collapsed for just these reasons. Certain soils, like the Kalahari and Benin sands of Africa carry good forest, but, if cleared, only two worthwhile crops can be grown. The luxuriance of tropical forest deceived many colonists from Europe, their efforts being commemorated by scrub and bare rock, nowhere more markedly than the 'Joden Savanna' of Surinam, the result of a short-lived farming attempt by Jewish refugees 150 years ago.

The traditional forest cultivators are now being joined in many parts of the world by subsistence peasants, new arrivals, pushing further and further into the forest, often along paths or tracks cut by lumbermen. In Peru, for example, people from the Andes are moving down and across as a front into the Amazon plain. It has been estimated that in the mid-1970s there were at least 140 million such people around the tropics occupying some two million square kilometres of the rain forest, about a fifth of its total area. They were converting the forest at a rate of some 100 000 square kilometres per annum. The greatest effect is in Indomalesia, where some 85 000 square kilometres are thought to be lost each year. In short, farming is reducing the rain forest by 1.5 % of its area annually. This rate is likely to increase as many of the countries with moist forests—Brazil, Colombia, Indonesia, Kenya, Madagascar, peninsular Malaysia, Peru, Philippines, Thailand, Uganda, Vietnam and all of West Africa and Central America— have high population growth rates. Furthermore, pressed by urban problems and sometimes apparently with other motives, several countries, such as Brazil, Colombia, Indonesia and Peru are promoting trans-migration schemes so that it is projected that the number of forest farmers could double or increase even more than that.

It has been argued that continuous agriculture could be maintained if a closed nutrient cycle could be achieved, the canopy not perforated so that leaching would be prevented and the forest floor would not deteriorate, nutrients added to equal those exported as crops and the diversity of species maintained. The problems to be added to this list of desiderata, making this theoretical model almost impossible to attain, include the problem of all year-round warmth, so that there is no respite from pests and diseases, a rapid breakdown of litter and subsequently enhanced leaching after the harvest of the crop. Furthermore, the social aspirations of the cultivators themselves in a climate where actual and potential production per man per year is less than in temperate countries (2), and such simple facts as the rapid rotting of produce, have to be taken into account. The mixture theory is also matched by the fact that, in practice, many crops have had their natural resistances, whether they be chemical or mechanical, or indeed temporal like staggered germination, bred out. The question then comes back to tackling the problem of how yield could be improved using traditional methods. Such ideas as the use of more legumes or other nitrogen-fixers and the ingenious use of nitrogen-fixing bacteria in the floating fern, *Azolla*, in paddy fields in southern China offer a ray of hope. Remarkable systems used by Chinese farmers in western Borneo merit further attention (1). Here grains, pepper and rubber and many vegetable crops are interspersed with fishponds and livestock grazing, enabling the people to make permanent use of impoverished soils.

Farming, then, is the biggest devourer of rain forest. Perhaps the region which has received most attention in the press in this context is Amazonia. Formerly the Amazon region was more thinly populated than the Sahara desert, containing perhaps some 50 000 people (3), and importing food. The government's plan was to cut a 70 m wide swathe through the forest for a major highway and that 100 km both sides of this was to be developed. Every poor family that moved there from the crowded east of Brazil was to have about 100 ha and a small house. There was to have been an 'agropolis' every 50 km and a 'ruropolis' every 150 km. All the colonists were supposed to feed themselves, though each of the plots was supposed to be left half-covered with forest. Such an idea led to isolated fragmentation of the forest, but in the ten years up to 1977 over 11 000 km of roads were built and a million settlers moved in. Land was given away and there were tax incentives to exploit the area, though increasingly it was large ranching projects and multinational interests that took more and more land. By 1977, then, there were 300 cattle ranches and 6 000 000 head of cattle, while a fifth of the forest had disappeared. The timber was burnt rather than used or sold. Such large companies as Volkswagen, which burnt down 120 000 ha, became involved. It was found that certain valuable cash crops like coffee, cocoa, oil palm and pepper grew well along rivers and that under the forest there was probably enough iron ore to meet world demand for 400 years (4), large deposits of bauxite, gold, nickel, copper and tin. The great Jari scheme, where four million hectares of land were bought along the Jari, a tributary of the Amazon, was planned to combine the mining and smelting of bauxite with the establishment of plantations for pulp, as a world shortage of paper was envisaged. Over 4500 km of roads, four towns, an airport, railway, a port, schools and hospitals were built, but the tree selected for the plantations, a species of *Gmelina* (Verbenaceae) from south-east Asia, failed. *Eucalyptus* and pines were tried but grew too slowly, and the whole enormous project has now been sold by the American businessman who set it up. The stress on mineral extraction has left the settlers (now almost 10 000 000 as was estimated early in 1982) in effect abandoned, and their fate is reported in terms of disputes over land, the sowing of their land with weed seeds from the air and even the poisoning of their drinking water.

9.1.2   *Logging and silviculture*

In 1974 (1), the world wood requirement was some 2500 million m³, of which some 47 % was used as fuel (80 % of it in the developing world), 43 % for building and other 'solid wood' purposes (two-thirds of this in the developed world) and 10 % for paper (some seven-eighths of this used in the developed world). It is estimated that the demand by the turn of the century will be 6000 million m³. So far, tropical moist forests provide little more than 10 % of the total wood used as solid wood and pulp, but as temperate forests become depleted or increasingly under pressure of the 'environmental' lobby to be managed for functions other than production, attention will inevitably be focused on the tropical resources. In 1950, 4.2 million m³ were exported to the developed world, in 1980 some 66 million m³, and this could be 95 million m³ by the end of the century. Even now exports surpass local consumption, and Japan takes over half of them. Until lately, her major source has been Indomalesia, which is the origin of some 75 % of the trade in tropical hardwoods.

Recently it has become possible to convert simultaneously wood chips of a hundred or more hardwood species into paper pulp, which is important, as it is estimated that paper consumption will increase more than that of timber. The average citizen in the developed world uses over 155 kg of paper per annum (325 kg in the United States), whereas in the developing world, the average citizen uses less than 5 kg. It is estimated that demand in the developing world will increase by some 2.75 times per citizen and that in the developed world some three times, so that the proportion consumed in the tropical world is going to increase. Some parts of the developed world, much of western Europe for example, are self-sufficient in pulp, but Japan is heavily dependent on foreign sources, which provide almost half her pulp.

At first, very few species were extracted for export. In South America, the mahoganies, *Swietenia* spp., were much sought after, so that today, they have suffered through genetic erosion to such an extent that often they are not worth exploiting, only those of poor form having been left in the forests to set seed. In other forests, only the greenheart, *Ocotea rodioei* (Lauraceae), was exploited, the rest of the forest unused. Today only some 50 of the thousands of species in the Amazon are commercially exploited, though up to 400 may have some value. Africa exports only 35, of which ten make up some 70 %. In Indomalesia, there is concentrated interest in fewer than 100 species with exports of twelve or so. It is remarkable that despite these low numbers of species, little is known of their biology and one, the sebastião-de-arruda, a well-known timber export from Brazil since the last century, has only lately (1978) been botanically identified and given a Latin name: *Dalbergia decipularis* (Leguminosae).

Because lianes often tie together several trees, the felling of one tree may lead to considerable damage to others, while logging tracks may take up to 10 % or even 30 % of the forest area. It is estimated that in south-east Asia, some third or two-thirds of the residual trees are damaged irreparably while up to a third of the area is left as bare ground, often compacted by the forestry machinery. Greater care in extraction would lead to a higher price of the timber. The effect on arboreal animals is largely to force them to leave logged forest and, as forests diminish, to promote their over-crowding. This is indicated by more frequent calling (5) and, in the orang-utan, to fewer young, as the secondary forest is less acceptable to the apes, which prefer the strangling figs of the 'primary' forest. Of ground-living mammals in Malaya over half of the species are forest animals and the elimination of the forest leads to the elimination of almost all the mammalian fauna, save a few rats. Added to this is the pressure from wild-life traders for skins, eggs, live birds and butterflies, much trafficking in which is now illegal, but nevertheless rampant.

With the advent of techniques for pulping mixtures of species, the diversity of the rain forest becomes less of a problem. Small areas can be exploited intensively and more and more may be capable of being processed; for example, one plant in New Guinea can now utilize wood from up to 200 species, including dead and defective trees, so that yields have already increased by some 300 %. On the other hand, desolation in these areas is total. It has been suggested that forest may regenerate when 200 m swathes are cut through forest and utilized thus, but others argue that plantations should follow such clearance. Until fairly recently, tropical silviculture has largely relied on natural regeneration. 'Refinement' or the reduction of competition from non-utilizable species, often leads to a considerable increase in the area occupied by the crop, so that once this is cut, there are lots of gaps for pioneers. Sometimes these are valuable, as in the case of *Funtumia elastica* (Apocynaceae) in Uganda, a source of rubber. Systems involving the repeated return to the forest and removal of the best trees are referred to as 'polycyclic'. These cause repeated damage to the forest, including saplings of desirable species, and lead to the problem of genetic erosion of the crop, and are also difficult to administer. When natural regeneration is difficult or inadequate, it may be supple-mented artificially by planting out nursery-raised trees—'enrichment'—in gaps, lines or groups. In most extreme cases, close planting may require the clear-felling of the forest. Pressures for increased production are forcing out the naturally regenerating forests as commercial propositions, though very specialized woods are difficult to grow otherwise.

Ecologically-based silviculture classifies the regeneration characteristics or syndromes into three major but overlapping categories, viz. (1) the pioneers (partially fire-tolerant) and the gapfillers (fire-sensitive), both incapable of establishment or growth in the shade, e.g. *Albizia*, *Tectona* (teak), *Ochroma* (balsa), *Macaranga*; (2) trees of the consolidation phase which are only capable of rapid growth when exposed, i.e. are light-demanding later in life, e.g. *Swietenia*, *Shorea*, *Triplochiton* (obeche), *Khaya*, *Carapa*; and (3) the trees which are shade-bearers throughout life and are incapable of rapid growth in the sun, e.g. *Ocotea*. The pioneering syndrome was discussed in Chapter 5, but in terms of silviculture, its important features are the relative longevity of seeds, the large annual growth increments—2–10 m in height (10 m in *Albizia falcatoria*), 10–20 cm in bole diameter—the shortlived nature of the tree and the light perishable wood. The second group has shorter seed longevity and rarer seeding, germination in the open in some or in the shade in others, trees living for 100–300 years and producing light to dark woods of medium weight. The last group is the least known: the trees grow very slowly, live at least 300 years and produce dark, heavy, close-grained wood, much of which is unusable.

The manipulation of forest successional cycles can be seen as the ecological basis of tropical silviculture. The first-stage trees are largely used for pulp, while the second-stage ones are the bulk of the tropical timber industry. Many of these timbers are referred to as 'mahogany' of which some 200 sorts, many not true mahoganies (Meliaceae) but with timber features like them, have been listed (6). The third-stage timbers have specialized, if any, uses. Notable is greenheart, used for locks and harbour fittings and ports, as in the Panama Canal, for it withstands sea water well.

Restrictions on silviculture in the tropics are most striking in the area of soil properties; for example, the pisolites of parts of West Africa are some 10 m deep with no obvious horizons and, although trees grow well at first, they later collapse and the removal of the forest leads to desolation resembling a gravel pit. Building on the experiences of mixed tree and herbaceous cropping, or agrisilviculture, elaborate ecologically-based schemes have been proposed, using a succession from grass and herb crops to shrubby and mixed perennial crops with an understorey of shade demanders. Such a system in Central America (7) begins with maize and beans followed by cassava and banana and palms, then cocoa with rubber and, finally, timber trees of the Meliaceae.

Plantations favour pioneers such as the pines, *Pinus kesiya* and *P. merkusii*, in the Indomalesian region. Plantations outyield by almost ten times managed 'natural' forest and these pines have a long fibre suitable for pulp, but hardwoods, notably *Eucalyptus* spp. yield higher total amounts of dry matter, and the most productive may yield up to twice that of the best pines. Much research is now directed to the vegetative propagation of high-yielding clones, despite the potential danger of growing genetically identical monocultures over wide areas. Though increasing rapidly, plantation (1) probably still occupies less than 18 million ha in the tropics, (about 15 % of the world's plantations) an area of the same order of magnitude as that lost to agriculture annually, and half of it is in Asia. 85 % of all such plantations are of pines, teak or *Eucalyptus*.

9.1.3 *Ranching*

Perhaps the most exploitative destruction of tropical forests is associated with the Latin American beef trade. Between 1950 and 1975 (1), pasture in Central America doubled, largely at the expense of forest, and, although the average local consumption declined, the number of head of cattle doubled. The surplus beef went to the United States. Between 1966 and 1978, some 80 000 km² of Brazil's forests disappeared in the formation of the ranches mentioned above. After the burning of the forest, pioneer trees appear and it is burnt again, and again the following year. The grass is then sown and it is periodically burnt thereafter to improve palatability (8). Thousands more ranches are planned and yet Brazil still imports beef. The low cost of the land and of labour makes the beef cost 25 % of that of United States produced beef, but, because the cattle are grass-fed, the beef is only useful for 'fast food', a booming business not only in the United States but increasingly so in Europe. As Brazil improves her financial standing *vis-à-vis* the developed world through this 'hamburger connection', she fells her forests to keep a few cents off the cost of this standardized, bland food.

9.1.4 *Fuel*

At present, only a small part of the fuel used in tropical countries is taken from tropical rain forest, little of it from 'primary' forest. Usually, it is gathered in scrub or secondary vegetation or local woodlots are utilized.

Nevertheless, local supplies may become exhausted and, with an increase in the use of charcoal, particularly in urban areas, forests far away are beginning to be affected. Thus forests far from Bangkok are being converted into charcoal, as are those of northwest Kenya for the Nairobi market. The reduction of fuel availability leads to the use of dung, some 400 million tons of which are burnt in Africa and Asia alone each year. On the face of it, this seems good, but it must be remembered that each ton used for fuel instead of as a fertilizer means a yield loss of some 50 kg in grain production, for example.

9.2   The prospects

In the tropical rain forests of the world, there is great variation in the level of exploitation. At present rates and with present plans, by 1990 there will be little of the rain forest left in Australia, Bangladesh, India, Sumatra and Sulawesi, peninsular Malaysia, Melanesia, the Philippines, Sri Lanka, Thailand, Vietnam, Central America, Madagascar, East or West Africa, through the depredations of timber extraction, farming (planned or not), population pressures, including transmigration schemes, and cattle ranching. By the year 2000, it is estimated that the rest of the forests of south-east Asia (except perhaps New Guinea) and large parts of Amazonia, could be converted to other uses; even before then, most of Brazil's Atlantic Strip, Colombia's rain forests and Ecuador's rich Pacific coast forests could be gone. By the end of the century, parts of Burma's lowland forests, the forests of New Guinea, much of Amazonia and of Cameroon could be cleared, though this is less certain. Less under pressure at present, though information is rather poor, are Brazil's western Amazonia, because it is wet and far from markets, French Guiana, Guyana and Surinam, where there is at present little population pressure, and this is also true of much of the Zaïre basin. There is a view that these could last into the next century.

In general, then, over the next few decades, the world will lose the bulk of the rain forest remaining today. Many thousands of species of plants and animals will become extinct. The explorers' account of the unending forests of the nineteenth century will seem as fabulous as mediaeval bestiaries. Politics and economics have heeded the advice of biologists and conservationists but little. Even where money could be made through tourism by conserving forests with their complement of birds and other animals which attract visitors, the animals have been shot and agriculture has encroached. This has led to the regazetting of boundaries and the

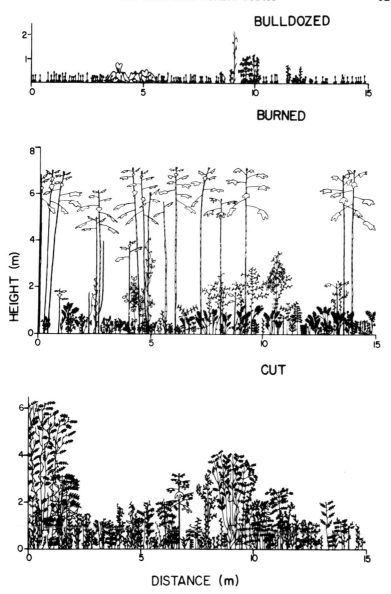

Figure 17   Profile diagrams representing the vegetation present in a 15 m × 1 m strip three years after the *caatinga* forest previously occupying the site had been cut (bottom), cut and burnt (middle), bulldozed clean (top). Reproduced with permission from C. Uhl *et al.* in *Oikos* **38** (1982) 315, Fig. 1.

F

diminishing of reserves. In this gloomy state of affairs, attention is being focused on the possibility of rehabilitation of habitats. This idea has borne some fruit in temperate countries, where spoil-tips, gravel-pits and other industrial eyesores have been returned to some sort of semblance of native vegetation with its associated fauna. What are the possibilities in the tropics?

In the Upper Rio Negro Region of southern Venezuela, a study on the recovery of *caatinga* forest was carried out (9). Two plots were cut and one of these was burnt after cutting. Shortly afterwards, an area nearby was bulldozed to make way for radar tracking equipment. The sites were re-examined (Fig. 17) three years after the initial disturbance, and recovery measured in terms of vegetation composition, biomass, nutrient accumulation, soil characteristics and nutrient leaching. The cut site was densely populated with many species of forest trees, the tallest of which had developed as coppice, while the burnt site had a loose canopy of pioneering *Cecropia* spp. 7 m tall, and the bulldozed site had a thin layer of herbs, notably *Xyris* sp. The nutrient levels in the soil were higher, even three years after disturbance, in both the cut and cut-and-burnt sites, than in the surrounding untouched forest, probably because of steady transfer of nutrients from the forest ash to the soil. In the bulldozed plots they were lowest of all, because the topsoil had been removed. The above-ground biomass in the cut site was $1291 \, \text{g/m}^2$, in the cut-and-burnt $879 \, \text{g/m}^2$, while in the bulldozed only $77 \, \text{g/m}^2$. From these figures, it was calculated that it would take some 100 years for the cut and cut-and-burnt sites to attain biomass levels of the original forest, while for the bulldozed forests, it is estimated that 1000 years would be needed.

Two forests in Costa Rica, one wet and one dry, also received cutting treatments (10). Biological features of the colonizing vegetation were seen to change with time and from the rate of change in these features a time for ecosystem recovery was calculated. Using mean seed-weight, which increases with time, as a parameter, it was found that the dry site would take about 150 years to revert to the conditions obtaining in the original forest, whereas in the wet forest, the figure of a thousand years was obtained once again. This is far longer than in temperate ecosystems.

9.2.1   Soils

Losses of soil through erosion vary greatly: under closed forest it may be 2.55 t per ha per annum in Trinidad, less than a tonne in Java or 0.41 in French Guiana, while under secondary forest in Madagascar it was nil, but up to 9 t when cleared and cultivated. Under *Eucalyptus* plantation it was 0.025 but, under other crops, up to 59 t (11). Loss of organic matter in the upper layers of the soil (7) was found to be at a rate of 9 % per annum in the first two years in Trinidad, while after clear-felling and burning in Ghana, up to 13 % was lost per annum and up to 33 % of the cations. On volcanic soils in the Solomon Islands, even higher figures have been recorded. In 22 years, croplands in Costa Rica lost 60 % of their calcium and 25 % of their magnesium even though the fields in the first year were higher than the surrounding forest in these ions, through ash input.

Interest has therefore been taken in the effect of adding fertilizer in an attempt at rehabilitation. In a study, again in Costa Rica (12), the vegetation biomass, nutrient content and species composition were measured during the first year after clear-cutting of plots, some of which were treated with commercial inorganic fertilizer (70 kg N, 87.5 kg P and 166 kg K per hectare) while others were planted with the pioneering *Cecropia obtusifolia*, as seedlings. These latter plots produced the highest biomass and nutrient standing crop while neither of these features was enhanced in similar plots which had been fertilized. The plots allowed to regenerate naturally were dominated by shrubs and trees on the unfertilized ones, though by herbs on those which had been fertilized. These latter had the lowest biomass and the lowest nutrient standing crop. In short, fertilization enhanced neither the build-up of biological materials nor the capture of nutrients by it. It merely retarded the successional process by enhancing the competitive ability of the herbs, in this case *Phytolacca rivinoides* (Phytolaccaceae). which dominated. A similar retardation has been recorded from Fiji where the fertilizer applied was some 195 kg P per hectare (13).

9.1.2   *The new vegetation*

If it could be ensured that there would be no further interference from man during the re-establishment of tropical rain forests, would the resultant forest actually resemble that which has been lost? All the evidence suggests otherwise. Abandoning of logged-over forest leads to the establishment of trees which develop their mature crown characteristics at a height much lower than that at which trees in closed forest do (14). Ng has calculated that height reductions of 25 or even 50 % can be expected. This leads to a vertical compression of forest structure and a reduction in the living space within the forest. This is already well known in temperate countries: trees established in parkland are shorter and with branches nearer the ground than in closed forest trees, and the 'bog-oaks' dug out of the fens of East Anglia show that the boles of the British oak forests of prehistory were much greater in size than any grown today. Even the great ecclesiastical buildings of the past incorporated such timbers taken from the relict forest surviving until the mediaeval period. Some documentary evidence survives in the form of paintings, notably by the Dutch and Flemish masters, who depicted the last of the spindly forest-grown giant trees of Europe as they disappeared.

Indeed, the modern clearing of the tropical forests is a continuation of the worldwide clear-felling initiated in the temperate regions. The removal of the Mediterranean forests in antiquity, much accelerated in recent times, and the clearing and desiccation of the region of the Tigris and Euphrates have had devastating effects on landscape and history. The cedars of Lebanon are a pathetic memorial to the lost vegetation. An example as recent as the late 1940s was the flora of the Mount Athos area in Greece, which was exposed to some 947 peasants and their 30 000 beasts for two years, in which time it was browsed off and twelve of the endemic plant species there have become extinct as a result.

9.1.3 *Conservation*

There are many arguments for conservation of the biological heritage of the world; in view of the immediate plight of much of humanity, in a local context there may also be many humane arguments against it. These have been well put elsewhere and here only some ecological arguments, which may bear repetition, will be reiterated.

In a world living with the possibility of instant Armageddon, generated by advances in the knowledge of atomic physics, the threat of devastation through slower biological processes is possibly heeded less than it might otherwise be. Nevertheless, one possible consequence of the removal of rain forest is frequently brought to the fore, namely the effect on the carbon dioxide balance of the earth's atmosphere and, thence, the possible warming of the earth through the 'greenhouse effect' leading to the melting of the icecaps and glaciers, with devastation in the form of flooding. What is the evidence for this potential 'eco-disaster'?

There is more carbon in tropical moist forest than there is in all temperate forests and cultivated land put together. The tropical forests (15) affect the carbon balance of the world by fixing large amounts of carbon at a rapid rate, by releasing it as carbon dioxide to the atmosphere through respiration, and exporting carbon as organic matter to the sea, to peat, or

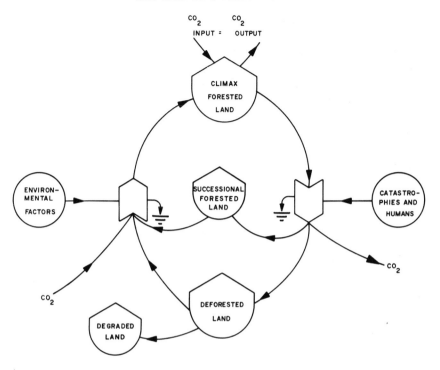

Figure 18   Flow diagram illustrating land-use changes that affect carbon cycling. Reproduced from *Unasylva* **32** n. 129 (1980) 11, courtesy FAO.

as forest products, largely timber. Those who argue that the forests are potential sources of carbon, believe that rapid rates of forest removal will increase the levels of carbon dioxide in the air through burning and decomposition of the vegetation. Those who argue the reverse, citing the rapid rates of succession and high carbon dioxide utilization of forest, believe that regenerating forests are a sink for carbon dioxide. A balanced view is provided by Fig. 18.

Carbon release to the atmosphere is deemed to increase with more drastic forms of land-use change, for the original forest is held to be in gaseous balance with the atmosphere. Some have argued that up to 95 % of the carbon in the forests is given up to the atmosphere in this way. The successional stages are the net consumers of carbon dioxide. When human beings are completely dependent on solar energy for survival, there is a stable steady-state with respect to atmospheric carbon, for then they are simple consumers using traditional shifting cultivation, hunting or gathering as a means of obtaining food. The activities of such human beings are not extensive enough to outweigh the effects of regeneration. This assumes that the mature forests are in equilibrium with the atmosphere. Evidence suggests that this is not always so, for such forests are not 'closed', and 'leak' small but measurable amounts of dissolved carbon to downstream vegetation. When extrapolated, such figures as 0.2×10^{14} g carbon per year exported from the Amazon are produced, though lately estimates for this figure have been raised fivefold. There are few such figures as yet and their significance is questionable, for it is not known how much of this carbon is lost irrevocably in the bottom of the seas and how much is respired back to the atmosphere by marine organisms.

It has been argued that those areas of the world relying on fossil fuels rather than on living forests and those where agriculture is less consumptive of land than formerly, as in Puerto Rico for example, may be net sinks of carbon, so that an assessment of the effect on carbon-balance has to include an assessment of land-use worldwide, not, then, a simple equation and, in short, we do not know the answer. Much more certain to be locally devastating is any drop in rainfall due to nearby forest removal.

In a time of world recession, demand for tropical timbers has declined. Some lumber companies have ceased operations in the tropical rain forest and some have even gone bankrupt. Thus the definition of what is a 'commercial' species changes with markets, or indeed with fashion, but this is only a temporary respite in one sector of the pressures on rain forest. Forest people have come sufficiently into contact with the ideas of the developed world and its values to be changed irrevocably. The animals are gone from many forests, which are changed in other ways as a consequence. It seems that the frequency of cyclonic storms is increasing in the tropics. In the longer term, the weather will change as the next ice age arrives, and ultimately the continents will change their orientation with respect to one another. In this world of inevitable change, what is the rationale of conservation if it has a basis beyond sentiment? When reduced to the minimum, it must surely be an effort to put a brake on accelerating universal change arising from the direct action of man, so that resources may be saved for later consumption. Unless unchecked, at least in some places, we lose not only what is labelled our 'heritage' but we lose its variety, possibly before the value of this variety can be assessed, both in terms of diversity valuable in itself, and the properties of the components of that diversity. The theme of this book is of change and diversity and no further remarks deliberately praising and encouraging conservation will be made here, for the readership of this book must be largely counted among the 'converted'. Given then that conservation is an essential part of the overall management of rain forests in the tropics, what should be top priority and how should it be conserved?

So far, a mere 2 % or so of tropical moist forests have been set aside under protected status, though often this is not more than a feature of government maps. Because of exceptional richness and also because they are severely threatened, Myers (16) has drawn up a list of top priority areas which include peninsular Malaysia, Madagascar and the relict coastal forest strip in Atlantic Brazil. Choosing what to concentrate on relies on a knowledge which may not yet be sufficiently deep to make decisions, but representative areas of at least eight main phytogeographical zones in Amazonia, the major forest types of Indomalesia and the different formations of the Zaïre basin in Africa would be a minimum. Some would argue that the Pleistocene refugia recognized in South America and posited elsewhere would serve as a basis, though this concept seems inapplicable to Indomalesia at least. The centres of diversity may not correspond with these supposed refugia and, even if they do, how big should preserved tracts be? The impossible task of estimating how large a population of rain-forest trees needs to be to be self-sustaining has meant that the minimum size for such reserves is not known accurately. In earlier chapters, the prevalence of dioecy, and the graduated rather than 'all-or-nothing' flowering response were stressed: these and the high degree of endemism of moist forest plants, compared with those of seasonal forest suggest that larger and larger reserves are required (14). Many relict forests kept as water catchment or for scientific interest are believed to be declining because they are too small. Small reserves are known to have increased tree fall at the margins and isolated pockets of forest with trees out of synchrony with the surroundings are likely to be targets for insect predation. Loss of fauna and lowering of humidity will prevent germination of many species. In Brazil an effort has been made to find the appropriate size and plots of 1, 10, 100, 1000 and 10 000 hectares have been set aside so that the decline in species numbers can be assessed more accurately (17).

Looking at Amazonia, then, Myers has estimated that the eight major phytogeographical regions and the sixteen centres of species diversity would require some 185 000 km^2 of reserves including buffer zones around them. This represents an area of about 80 % as large as Great Britain. By 1981, some reserves had been established, but so far they are far from enough. Furthermore, if the stress is laid on the areas thought to be important in currently fashionable ecological thinking, the areas which are of importance in terms of water-catchment may be neglected. This would have disastrous effects not only on the inhabitants of Amazonia, but also on the pieces of forest conserved, for these would be greatly affected by being left in a sea of desiccated landscape (16). Nevertheless, there are plans for the setting aside of some $625\,000\,km^2$ of forest around the tropical world. This represents well over 7 % of the whole biome but falls short of the 10–20 % required by certain theorists. But, as Myers points out, those countries in the developing tropical world are being asked, for the good of mankind, to set aside a tenth of their land surface. How would such a request be received in a developed country?

The reasons for conservation of rain forest have been set out by Myers (16) as follows:

1. To allow evolutionary processes to continue
2. To safeguard the role of the moist forests in regulating the biosphere, especially in maintaining climatic stability—local, regional and maybe even global
3. To provide a stock of plants and animals for pure and applied research
4. To provide undisturbed (sic) ecosystems for benchmark monitoring in comparison with which land-use strategies for the forest can be evaluated
5. To conserve gene pools of plants and animals for their future use to man and for maintaining ecosystem stability
6. To safeguard watersheds to prevent flooding and soil erosion and to maintain water supplies
7. To provide wildlands for recreation, for enjoyment and for education
8. To provide local income and foreign exchange through tourism.

Many of these have been touched on in the foregoing chapters, while others are beyond the scope of a book such as this. One, which has not been mentioned and may prove to be of the greatest importance, is the significance of many 'minor' forest products, that is, those other than timber. It must be borne in mind that trade in these commodities long antedates that in timber, the commercial extraction of which in the tropics is a relatively modern development (18). Second to timber in commercial importance in S.E. Asia today is the rattan industry, based on the stems of climbing palms. Many other species, especially plants, have made thousands of contributions to modern agriculture, to medicine and to industry (16). Such include vincristine, a drug which has quadrupled the chance of recovery for children suffering from leukaemia, anti-cancer drugs and compounds that combat heart disease, while many believe that the anti-fertility drugs used by forest people may have great potential as contraceptives. Attention is also focused on the possible exploitation of the West African plants, *Thaumatococcus daniellii* (Marantaceae), *Synsepalum dulciferum* (Sapotaceae) and *Dioscoreophyllum cumminsii* (Menispermaceae) as sources for synthetic sweeteners (19). Some trees and other plants may produce enough alcohol or oils suitable for petroleum substitutes. Despite trading in gums and rubber and a hundred other forest products for centuries, the world has not screened 99% of plant species from rain forests. Already, though, some forest plants, utilized in a 'minor' way, are endangered, like *Garcinia epunctata* and *G. kola* (Guttiferae), used as chewing sticks in W. Africa, and now becoming rare (19).

In the world as a whole, some 3000 species of plant have been grown at one time or another for food. Of these, some 150 have been grown on a commercial scale, though the world is now largely reliant on about twenty. Some of these are genetically rather uniform and with few known wild relations. The tropics are experiencing increased levels of attack from pests and diseases while one in ten of all plant species has recently become extinct or is in danger of becoming so. Many of these latter (14) persist only in small numbers of mature individuals with little possibility of regenerating and multiplying *in situ*. For these, their evolutionary life in the rain forest is at an end: if they are to be saved, for whatever reason, seeds must be collected for arboreta and gardens. In the last century, a triumph was the spreading of commercially important crop plants, such as rubber, through the agency of botanic gardens. Their role in an ever more quickly changing world becomes clear and it is heartening to see that such an organization as the Royal Botanic Gardens at Kew, with its old connections in the tropical world, has set up such a system of seedbanks and information.

In a much broader context, Poore (20) has put the least disturbed rain forests in his simplified scheme of worldwide land-use categories as 'natural', compared with 'transformed', where the original vegetation has been largely removed and replaced by an artificial system, and 'modified' where the land is being changed by human use, but which still holds naturally occurring plants and animals, having some continuity with the original. The 'natural' ecosystems are now largely confined to remote or inaccessible regions, where neither agriculture nor commercial forestry is economically possible, though such places are now under other pressures— mineral exploitation or tourism, for example—while others are getting cut off as islands in seas of other types of land-use even if they are conserved. They may represent some 2.5% of the world's land area whereas 11% is under agriculture and less than 1 % under plantation forestry. This leaves over 80 % of the 'modified' lands, which receive little attention from the agriculturist because they are 'marginal', or from conservationists in the tropics, though it is, of course, such lands that are those being most vociferously fought over in the greatly modified landscapes of northern Europe, for example. Furthermore, mismanagement here will affect both the 'natural' and 'transformed'.

There are very strong pressures in many parts of the world to intensify the use and improve the efficiency of the transformed ecosystems: this receives universal acclaim, for these ecosystems contribute to satisfying the world's rising requirements for food and other raw materials. They are profitable, modern and provide outlets for products of technology and industry: they respond to the human instincts to be tidier, more up-to-date and more productive than one's neighbour. In other parts of the world with higher percentages of agricultural workers, however, the introduction of even modest improvements can lead to rural unemployment and migration to the urban slums, so that much of the developing world would not, contrary to much in aid programmes, welcome such innovation in the long run. Nevertheless, in many parts of the world, the intensive use of such systems may be the only relief of the pressure on other less transformed ones, such that it can be argued that research in agriculture should be stepped up as an aid to conservation (21).

POSTSCRIPT

The one big lesson of the study of tropical ecology must surely be that concepts derived from purely temperate studies are often too rigid in definition, or, at least, with too great an emphasis on one or a few particular aspects, to be of universal application. This is as true for morphology, as was first perceived by Alexander's army confronted with aerial roots in India, as it is for evolutionary and taxonomic studies in the light of rampant parallelism and ochlospecies, and ecology, which is now facing a relaxing of the concepts of pollination 'syndromes', tightly co-evolved dispersal mechanisms, the course of successional cycles, forest stratification and the nature of the coexistence of species. The relaxing of the straitjacket allows us to look afresh at temperate ecology in a world context as was advocated for the British flora long ago by A. H. Church (1).

Morphology and taxonomy were the bases of biology and were followed by physiology and biochemistry. The first two, in the light of tropical work, are advancing. As yet, the diversity of physiology and biochemistry of tropical plants is by comparison, little investigated. Very probably, though, a broadening of concepts will follow such investigations, as it has in cytology where the sweeping statements of chromosomal uniformity in tree groups seem absurd, now that variation as great as in temperate herbs has been found in tropical tree groups (2). In the area of genetics, even the most sacred of cows, the importance of cross-fertilization, has been called into question, as has the whole dogma of speciation involving populations rather than individuals (3), again, from a consideration of tropical organisms. To be honest, we know little about the biological world in all its diversity and this is a point that is rarely made in textbooks. There has

135

been an effort, understandable enough, to draw up schemes and discover 'laws', possibly in an attempt to imitate essentially different physical sciences.

Ecology cannot be studied in isolation from evolution, biogeography or taxonomy, and the circumscription of the 'subject' is bound to be vague. To many scientists, then, ecology seems woolly and scarcely respectable: in many ways it is nearer economics than other sciences such as physics. When integrated with its sister disciplines, patterns do emerge, however, and some sense can be made of them (4). It is heartening to see that recent tropical work, for example, is increasingly imbued with a better taxonomic base than hitherto.

It will not have escaped the reader's notice that, in this book, many examples have been taken from the tree family, Meliaceae: this is not merely because it has had the effect of loading the text with fewer plant names (nor just because the author happens to be studying them) but it demonstrates that within such a family, a great diversity of form and ecology can be found. The Meliaceae are not unique in this respect, for their architecture and relationships with animals are paralleled again and again in other groups. Indeed, the parallelisms in the different groups of angiosperms in terms of pioneers or rheophytes are as striking as the far better-known zoological examples of marsupial and placental mammal parallelisms. This brings us back to a consideration of the importance of 'form' and the potential within particular groups for diversification. Why do, for example, the nutmegs and their allies, Myristicaceae, all have very similar seeds (arillate) and the same architectural model, whereas Euphorbiaceae are variable in almost all features and pervade temperate as well as tropical regions, unlike the Myristicaceae, bound to the rain forest?

Parallelisms underline the importance of historical considerations, in that organisms are not evenly spread and completely mixed throughout the tropics. The paucity of species of bees in south-east Asia or of palms in Africa must have a historical explanation just as the importance of Wallace's Line and the isthmus of Panama have such explanations. Furthermore, it is unreasonable to suppose that species are not still extending their ranges, or indeed succumbing to those that are. Also, species are still in the making, and the frustrating variation patterns of certain tree species, for example, may mirror just this. Moreover, there must be caution, for the distributions may have been affected further by man as, for example, the bird-fanciers of pre-Columbian America, or those transporting crops including trees, such as *Ceiba pentandra*. As we have seen, these may appear very much 'at home' and very aggressive in their new environments; so much so that weeds like *Lantana camara* (Verbenaceae), native to America, may completely arrest succession in the Old World.

The importance of time in terms of the asynchrony of the spread or extinction of associated organisms, such as dispersal agents in the case of certain Central American trees discussed in Chapter 7 and thus that of the concept of anachronistic traits in organisms, leads to a consideration of the wisdom or otherwise of viewing organisms in terms of their constituent features rather than viewing them as ragbags of compromise and opportunism. Again, with time, the disappearance of the large mammals from many tropical forests is certainly going to have a great effect, but with the exception of tree species that seem to be exclusively elephant-dispersed and similar examples, that effect may not be a specific, but a general, one. In Africa, the removal of these animals has accelerated in recent years such that the diversified mosaic landscapes maintained by what Kortlandt (5) has called the 'bulldozer herbivores', may be greatly modified. In turn, the great diversity of such faunas seems to argue that formerly rain forest areas may have been more diverse in their structure, which might well have an effect on the interpretation of vegetation history. Certainly these animals must have had some considerable effect through their foraging, debarking, uprooting, digging and trampling.

Ecology is concerned with the balance of a range of influences, and only rarely can one such influence or factor be recognized as having overriding importance. This has great implications for conservation. The type of forest that returns after complete clearance is different not only in terms of its height, but also its constituents. It has been estimated (6) that in Central Borneo, dipterocarps may spread at an average rate of 2 m per annum and that rivers may be a major obstacle to reinvasion. In the rehabilitation of forest, then, old trees should be left to act as seed sources (7) but management of tropical high forest is such that foresters (8) are now beginning to question whether there are any really successful examples of long-term sustainable management of such forest for timber production, or, indeed, whether it is practicable at all. Again, we are faced with a problem, here a very practical one which seems not to go away even when veiled in figures of biomass, turnover rates or basal areas.

Almost forty years ago, Corner (9) drew biologists' attention to what needed to be done in improving knowledge of tropical rain forest. Painfully little of what he suggested has been achieved. Still recommendations pour forth for survey and collecting material, preparation of inventories, just what ecologists and taxonomists before them have been trying to do for two centuries (10). As Heywood has put it: 'Today when we have powerful tools for the study of phylogeny, such as numerical cladistics, and powerful new classes of data, such as amino-acid sequences of cytochrome C and plastocyanins, we are in a situation where we have to consider seriously whether we should concentrate our energies and resources on floristic exploration and writing Floras and monographs'. Indeed we are.

FURTHER READING

Ewel, J. (ed.) Tropical succession. *Biotropica* **12**(2) suppl., 1980.
Flenley, J. R. *The Equatorial Rain Forest: a Geological History.* Butterworth, London, 1979.
Grainger, A. The state of the world's tropical forests. *Ecologist* **10**, 1–54 (1980).
Grubb, P. J. The maintenance of species-richness in plant communities. The importance of the regeneration niche. *Biological Reviews* **52**, 107–145 (1977).
Hallé, F., Oldeman, R. A. A. and Tomlinson, P. B. *Tropical Trees and Forests. An Architectural Analysis.* Springer, Berlin, 1978.
Janzen, D. H. *Ecology of Plants in the Tropics.* Arnold, London, 1975.
Longman, K. A. and Jenik, J. *Tropical Forest and its Environment.* Longman, 1974.
Meggers, B. J., Ayensu, E. S. and Duckworth, W. D. (eds.) *Tropical Rain Forest Ecosystems in Africa and South America: a Comparative Review.* Smithsonian Institution, Washington, 1973.
Myers, N. *The Conversion of Moist Tropical Forests.* National Academy of Sciences, Washington, 1980.
Richards, P. W. *The Tropical Rain Forest.* Cambridge University Press, 1952 (with later reprints).
Riehl, H. *Climate and Weather in the Tropics.* Academic Press, London, 1979.
Tomlinson, P. B. and Zimmermann, M. H. (eds.) *Tropical Trees as Living Systems.* Cambridge University Press, 1978.
Whitmore, T. C. *Tropical Rain Forests of the Far East.* Clarendon Press, Oxford, 1975.

From the references which follow, the reader will see that to keep abreast of developments in the subject, it is valuable to read new issues of certain journals, such as *Acta amazonica, American Naturalist, Biotropica, Ecology, Evolution, Malaysian Forester, Oikos.*

REFERENCES

Chapter 1 (pp. 1–13)
1. Stearn, W. T. *Gdns' Bull., Sing.* **29** (1977), 13–18.
2. Goodland, R. J. *Oikos* **26** (1975), 240–245.
3. Ewel, J. (ed.) Tropical succession. *Biotropica* **12** (2) (Suppl.), 1980.
4. Myers, N. *The Conversion of Tropical Moist Forests*. Nat. Acad. Sci., Washington, 1980.
5. Dawson, J. W. *Biotropica* **12** (1980), 159–160.
6. Whitmore, T. C. *Tropical Rain Forests of the Far East*. Clarendon Press, Oxford, 1975, p. 4, etc.
7. Opler, P. A. *et al.* in J. Cairns *et al., Recovery and Restoration of Damaged Ecosystems*. Univ. Press Virginia, Charlottesville, 1977, pp. 379–421.
8. *The Times*, 27 June 1980.
9. Janzen, D. H. *Ecology of Plants in the Tropics*. Edward Arnold, London, 1975.

Chapter 2 (pp. 14–23)
1. Howarth, M. K. and Adams, C. G. in L. R. M. Cocks (ed.), *The Evolving Earth*. British Museum (Natural History) and Cambridge Univ. Press, 1981, pp. 197–220, 221–236.
2. Ashton, P. S. *Gdns' Bull., Sing.* **29** (1977), 19–23.
3. Hallé, F., Oldeman, R. A. A. and Tomlinson, P. B. *Tropical Trees and Forests. An Architectural Analysis*. Springer, Berlin, 1978.
4. Whitmore, T. C. (ed.) *Wallace's Line and Plate Tectonics*. Clarendon Press, Oxford, 1981.
5. Hall, J. B. and Swaine, M. D. *Distribution and Ecology of Vascular Plants in a Tropical Rain Forest*. Junk, The Hague etc., 1981; Morley, R. J. *J. Biogeogr.* **8** (1981), 383–404.
6. Longman, K. A. and Jeník, J. *Tropical Forest and its Environment*. Longman, London, 1974.
7. Manokaran, N. *Malays. For.* **42** (1979), 174–201.
8. Sugden, A. M. *J. Arnold Arb.* **62** (1982), 1–61.
9. Jordan, C. F. *et al. Acta Amaz.* **11** (1981), 87–92.
10. Dean, J. M. and Smith, A. P. *Biotropica* **10** (1978), 152–154.
11. Riehl, H. *Climate and Weather in the Tropics*. Academic Press, London, 1979.
12. Lee, D. W. *et al. Biotropica* **11** (1979), 70–77.

Chapter 3 (pp. 24–35)
1. Harcombe, P. A. in J. Ewel (ed.) Tropical succession. *Biotropica* **12** (2) (Suppl.), 1980, pp. 8–15.

140   TROPICAL RAIN FOREST ECOLOGY

2. Burnham, C. P. in Whitmore, T. C. *Tropical Rain Forests of the Far East*. Clarendon Press, Oxford, 1975, Chapter 9.
3. Anderson, A. B. *Biotropica* **13** (1981), 199–201.
4. Buckley, R. C. *et al. Biotropica* **12** (1980), 124–136; van Steenis, C. G. G. J. *Bot. J. Linn. Soc.* **79** (1979), 97–178.
5. Golley, F. B. *et al. Biotropica* **10** (1978), 144–151.
6. Hardy, F. *Biotropica* **10** (1978), 71–72.
7. Jordan, C. *Ecology* **63** (1982), 647–654.
8. Jordan, C., *et al. Biotropica* **12** (1980), 61–66.
9. Tukey, H. B., in Odum, H. T. and Pigeon, R. F. (eds.), *A Tropical Rain Forest*. U. S. Atomic Energy Commission, Tennessee, 1970, Chapter H-11.
10. Witkamp, M. *Ibid.*, Chapter H-14.
11. Williamson, G. B. *Biotropica* **13** (1981), 228–231.
12. Enright, N. J. *Malays. For.* **42** (1979), 202–207.
13. Weigert, R. G. and Murphy, P. in Odum, H. T. and Pigeon, R. F. (eds.), *A Tropical Rain Forest*. U. S. Atomic Energy Commission, Tennessee, 1970, Chapter H-5.
14. Lang, G. E. and Knight, D. H. *Biotropica* **11** (1979), 316–317.
15. Dudgeon, D. *Symposium—The Tropical Rain Forest*, Poster Abstracts. Leeds, 1982.*
16. Jordan, C. and Herrera, R. *Amer. Nat.* **117** (1981), 167–180.
17. Redhead, J. F. and Bowen, G. D., in Mikola, P. (ed.), *Tropical Mycorrhiza Research*. Clarendon Press, Oxford, 1980, Chapters 16, 21.
18. Allen, O. N. and Allen, E. K. *The Leguminosae*. Macmillan, London, 1981.
19. Janos, D. P. *Symposium—The Tropical Rain Forest*, Abstracts. Leeds, 1982.
20. Manokaran, N. *Malays. For.* **43** (1980), 266–289.
21. Jordan, C. F. and Medina, E. *Ann. Mo. bot. Gdn.* **64** (1977), 737–745.

* The papers presented at this symposium are to be published in 1983.

Chapter 4 (pp. 36–52)
1. Drury, W. H. and Nisbet, I. C. T. *J. Arnold Arb.* **54** (1973), 331–368.
2. Hallé, F., Oldeman, R. A. A. and Tomlinson, P. B. *Tropical Trees and Forests. An Architectural Analysis*. Springer, Berlin, 1978.
3. Mabberley, D. J. in Bramwell, D. (ed.) *Plants and Islands*. Academic Press, London, 1979, pp. 259–277.
4. Tho, Y. P., *Malays. For.* **45** (1982), 184–192.
5. Rijksen, H. D., *Meded. Landb. Wageningen* 78-2 (1978).
6. Poore, M. E. D. *J. Ecol.* **56** (1968), 143–196.
7. Whitmore, T. C. *Tropical Rain Forests of the Far East*. Clarendon Press, Oxford, 1975.
8. Hartshorn, G. S., in Tomlinson, P. B. and Zimmermann, M. H. *Tropical Trees as Living Systems*. Cambridge University Press, 1978, pp. 617–638.
9. Ewel, J. (ed.) Tropical succession. *Biotropica* **12** (2) (Suppl.), 1980.
10. Putz, F. *Symposium—The Tropical Rain Forest*, Poster Abstracts. Leeds, 1982.
11. Cheke, A. S. *et al. Biotropica* **11** (1979), 88–95.
12. Ng, F. S. P., in Tomlinson, P. B. and Zimmermann, M. H. *Tropical Trees as Living Systems*. Cambridge University Press, 1978, pp. 129–162.
13. Whitmore, T. C. and Hartshorn, G. S. *ibid.*, pp. 617–638, 639–655.
14. Whitmore, T. C. *ibid.*,
15. Hall, J. B. and Swaine, M. D. *Distribution and Ecology of Vascular Plants in a Tropical Rain Forest*. Junk, The Hague etc., 1981.
16. Kochummen, K. M. and Ng, F. S. P. *Malays. For.* **40**, (1977), 61–78.
17. Gómez-Pompa, A. and Vázquez-Yanes, C. in West, D. C. *et al.* (eds.), *Forest Succession. Concepts and applications*. Springer, New York, 1981, pp. 246–266.
18. Janzen, D. H. *Biotropica* **10** (1978), 121.

19. Brokaw, N. *Symposium—The Tropical Rain Forest*, Poster Abstracts. Leeds, 1982.
20. Yeaton, R. *Biotropica* **11** (1979), 155–158.
21. Kenworthy, J. B. and Riswan, S. *Symposium—The Tropical Rain Forest*, Poster Abstracts, Leeds, 1982.
22. Primack, R. B. and Chai, P. *ibid.*
23. Schemske, D. W. and Brokaw, N. *Ecology*, **62** (1981), 938–945.
24. Flenley, J. *Symposium—The Tropical Rain Forest*, Poster Abstracts. Leeds, 1982.
25. Mabberley, D. J. *New Phytol.* **74**, (1975) 365–374.
26. Sugden, A. M. *J. Arnold Arb.* **62** (1982), 1–61; *Biotropica* **14** (1982), 208–219.
27. Ball, E. and Glucksman, J. *Proc. Roy. Soc. Lond.* (B) **190** (1975), 421–447.

Chapter 5 (pp. 53–79)
1. Thorne, R. F., in Meggers, B. J., Ayensu, E. S. and Duckworth, W. D. (eds.) *Tropical Rain Forest Ecosystems in Africa and South America: A Comparative Review*. Smithsonian Inst. Washington, 1973, p. 27–47.
2. Koechlin, J., in Richard-Vindard, G. and Battistini, R. (eds.) *Biogeography and Ecology in Madagascar*. Junk, The Hague, 1972, pp. 145–190.
3. Bourlière, F., in Meggers, B. J. *et al., op. cit.,* pp. 279–292; Janzen, D. H. *Ann. Mo bot. Gdn* **64** (1977), 706–736; Michener, C. D. *Ann. Mo bot. Gdn* **66** (1979), 277–347.
4. Sutton, S., *Symposium—The Tropical Rain Forest*. Abstracts. Leeds, 1982.
5. Hall, J. B. and Swaine, M. D. *Distribution and Ecology of Vascular Plants in a Tropical Rain Forest*. Junk, The Hague, etc., 1981.
6. Mitchell, A. W. *Reaching the Rain Forest Roof*. Leeds Phil. Soc., Leeds, 1982.
7. Hallé, F., Oldeman, R. A. A. and Tomlinson, P. B. *Tropical Trees and Forests. An Architectural Analysis*. Springer, Berlin, 1978.
8. Hallé, F. and Mabberley, D. J. *Gdns' Bull., Sing.* **29**, (1977), 175–181.
9. Mabberley, D. J. *Gdns' Bull., Sing.* **29**, (1977), 41–55.
10. Horn, H. S. *Scient. Amer.* **232** (5) (1975), 90–98.
11. Smith, A. P. *Biotropica* **11** (1979), 159–160.
12. Bodley, J. D. and Benson, F. C. *Biotropica* **12** (1980), 67–71.
13. Huxley, C. *New Phytol.* **80** (1978), 231–268.
14. Benzing, D. H. *Symposium—The Tropical Rain Forest*. Abstracts. Leeds, 1982.
15. Burtt, B. .L. *Gdns' Bull., Sing.* **29** (1977), 73–80.
16. van Steenis, C. G. G. J. *Rheophytes of the World*. Sijthoff & Noordhoff, Alphen aan den Rijn, 1981.
17. Mabberley, D. J. *Bull. Brit. Mus. (Nat. Hist.) Bot.* **6** (1979), 301–386.
18. Mabberley, D. J. *Taxon*, in press (1983).
19. Putz, F. *Malays. For.* **42** (1979), 1–24.
20. Croat, T. B. *Flora of Barro Colorado Island*. Stanford Univ. Press, Stanford, 1978.
21. Yap, S. K. *Malays. For.* **45** (1982), 21–35.
22. Ng, F. S. P. *Malays. For.* **40** (1977), 126–137.
23. Ng, F. S. P. and Loh, H. S. *Malays. For.* **37** (1974), 127–132.
24. Janzen, D. H. in Burley, J. and Styles, B. T. (eds.) *Tropical Trees. Variation, Breeding and Conservation*. Academic Press, London, 1976, pp. 179–188.
25. Corner, E. J. H. *Wayside Trees of Malaya*. 2 vols. Singapore, 1940.
26. Diamond, A. W. *Symposium—The Tropical Rain Forest*. Poster Abstracts. Leeds, 1982.

Chapter 6 (pp. 80–90)
1. Rosen, B. R., in Forey, P. L. (ed.) *The Evolving Biosphere*. British Museum and Cambridge Univ. Press, 1981, pp. 103–130.
2. Simpson, B. B. and Hoffer, J. *Ann. Rev. Ecol. Syst.* **9** (1978), 497–518.
3. Keel, S. H. K. and Prance, G. T. *Acta Amaz.* **9** (1979), 645–655.
4. Hubbell, S. P., *Symposium—The Tropical Rain Forest*. Abstracts. Leeds, 1982.

5. Huston, M. *J. Biogeogr.* **7** (1980), 147–157.
6. Snow, D. W. *Oikos* **15** (1965), 274–281.
7. Fleming, T. H. and Heithaus, E. R. *Biotropica* **13**, Suppl. (1981), 45–53.
8. Kiltie, R. A. *Biotropica* **13** (1981), 141–145.
9. Gillett, J. B. *Syst. Assoc. Publ.* **4** (1962), 37–46.
10. Hubbell, S. P. *Oikos* **35** (1980), 214–229.
11. Grubb, P. J. *Biol. Rev.* **52** (1977), 107–145.
12. Prance, G. T. and Mori, S. A. *Brittonia* **30** (1978), 21–33.
13. Richards, P. and Williamson, G. B. *Ecology* **56** (1975), 1226–1229.
14. Tanner, E. V. J. *Biol. J. Linn. Soc.* **18** (1982), 263–278.
15. Whitmore, T. C. *Commonw. For. Inst. Pap.* **46** (1974).
16. Sugden, A. M., *Symposium—The Tropical Rain Forest.* Abstracts. Leeds, 1982.
17. Brünig, E. F. and Klinge, H. *Gdns' Bull., Sing.* **29** (1977), 81–101.

Chapter 7 (pp. 91–109)

1. Bawa, K. S. *International Botanical Congress.* Abstracts. Sydney, 1981.
2. Eastop, V. F., in Forey, P. L. (ed.) *The Evolving Biosphere.* British Museum (Natural History) and Cambridge Univ. Press, 1981, pp. 179–190.
3. Appanah, S. *Malays. For.* **44** (1981), 37–42.
4. Yap, S. K. *Malays. For.* **45** (1982), 21–35.
5. Baker, H. G., in Tomlinson, P. B. and Zimmermann, M. H. (eds.) *Tropical Trees as Living Systems.* Cambridge Univ. Press, 1978, pp. 57–82.
6. Guerrant, E. O. and Fiedler, P. L., *Biotropica* **13**, Suppl. (1981), 25–33.
7. Snow, D. W., in Forey, P. L. (ed.) *op. cit.* pp. 169–178.
8. Bolten, A. B. and Feinsinger, P. *Biotropica* **10** (1978), 307–309; Pyke, G. H. and Waser, N. M. *Biotropica* **13** (1981), 260–270.
9. Hudson, P. and Sugden, A. M. *Symposium—The Tropical Rain Forest.* Poster Abstracts. Leeds, 1982.
10. Marshall, A. G. *ibid.*
11. Hopkins, H. *Symposium—The Tropical Rain Forest.* Abstracts. Leeds, 1982.
12. Janson, C. H. *et al. Biotropica* **13**, Suppl. (1981), 1–6.
13. Wheelwright, N. T. and Orians, C. H. *Amer. Nat.* **119** (1982), 402–413.
14. Howe, H. F. and de Steven, D. *Oecologia* **39** (1979), 185–196.
15. Leighton, M. and Leighton, D. *Symposium—The Tropical Rain Forest.* Abstracts. Leeds, 1982.
16. Croat, T. B. *Flora of Barro Colorado Island.* Stanford Univ. Press, Stanford, 1978.
17. Sazima, I. *et al. Symposium—The Tropical Rain Forest.* Poster Abstracts. Leeds, 1982.
18. Cont, J. G. H. *Biotropica* **11** (1979), 122.
19. Howe, H. F. *Ecology* **61** (1980), 944–959.
20. Ashton, P. S. in *Tropical Forest Ecosystems.* UNESCO, Paris, 1978. pp. 180–215.
21. Snow, D. W. *Biotropica* **13** (1981), 1–14.
22. Milton, K. *et al. Ecology* **63** (1982), 752–762.
23. Estrada, A. *Symposium—The Tropical Rain Forest.* Poster Abstracts. Leeds, 1982.
24. Mackinnon, J. *Anim. Behav.* **22** (1974), 3–74; Rijksen, H. D. *Meded. Landb. Wageningen* 78-2 (1978).
25. Hopkins, H. *Symposium—The Tropical Rain Forest.* Abstracts. Leeds, 1982.
26. Janzen, D. H. and Martin, P. S. *Science* **215** (1982), 19–27.
27. Dawkins, R. *The Extended Phenotype.* Freeman, Oxford, 1982, pp. 35 *et seq.*
28. Mabberley, D. J. *New Phytol.* **75** (1975), 289–295.
29. Corner, E. J. H. *The Natural History of Palms.* Weidenfeld & Nicolson, London, 1966.
30. Gottsteyer, G. *Biotropica* **10** (1978), 170–183.
31. Horvitz, C. C. and Beattie, A. J. *Amer. J. Bot.* **67** (1980), 321–326.

32. Alexandre, D.-Y. *La Terre et la Vie* **32** (1978), 47–62; Temple, S. A. *Science* **197** (1977), 885–886.
33. Wint, G. R. W. *Symposium—The Tropical Rain Forest*. Abstracts. Leeds, 1982.
34. Lieberman, D. and Lieberman, M. *Symposium—The Tropical Rain Forest*. Poster Abstracts. Leeds, 1982.
35. Lemen, C. *Oikos* **36** (1981), 65–67.
36. Cherrett, J. M. *Symposium—The Tropical Rain Forest*. Abstracts. Leeds, 1982.
37. Janzen, D. H. *Ecology of Plants in the Tropics*. Arnold, London, 1975.
38. Stout, J. *Biotropica* **11** (1979), 307–311.
39. Janzen, D. H., in Rosenthal, G. A. and Janzen, D. H. (eds.) *Herbivores and their Interaction with Secondary Plant Metabolites*. Academic Press, London, 1979, pp. 331–350.
40. McKey, D. B. *et al. Biol. J. Linn. Soc.* **16** (1981), 115–146.
41. Owen, D. F. *Oikos* **35** (1980), 230–235; Petelle, M. *Oikos* **38** (1982), 125–127.
42. Dickinson, T. A. and Tanner, E. V. J. *Biotropica* **10** (1978), 231–233.
43. Oldroyd, H. *The Natural History of Flies*. Weidenfeld & Nicolson, London, 1964, p. 84.

Chapter 8 (pp. 110–115)
1. Repenning, C. A. and Fejfar, O. *Nature* **299** (1982), 344–347.
2. Church, A. H. in Mabberley, D. J. (ed.) *Revolutionary Botany*. Clarendon Press, Oxford, 1981, pp. 237–245.
3. Rijksen, H. D. *Meded. Landb. Wageningen* 78–2 (1978); Whitmore, T. C. *Tropical Rain Forests of the Far East*. Clarendon Press, Oxford, 1975.
4. Corner, E. J. H., in *UNESCO Symposium on the impact of man on the humid tropics vegetation*. Canberra, 1962, pp. 38–41.
5. Lowenstein, F. W., in Meggers, B. J., Ayensu, E. S. and Duckworth, W. D. (eds.), *Tropical Rain Forest Ecosystems in Africa and South America: A Comparative Review*. Smithsonian Inst., Washington, 1973, pp. 293–310.
6. Purseglove, J. *Tropical Crops*, vol. 1. Longman, London, 1968, p. 12.
7. Meggers, B. J., in Meggers, B. J. *et al. op. cit.*, pp. 311–334.
8. Carey, I. *Orang asli*. Oxford Univ. Press, Kuala Lumpur, 1976.
9. Myers, N. *The Conversion of Moist Tropical Forests*. Nat. Acad. Sci., Washington, 1980.
10. Haemig, P. D. *Biotropica* **10** (1978), 11–17; **11** (1979), 81–87.

Chapter 9 (pp. 116–134)
1. Myers, N. *The Conversion of Moist Tropical Forests*. Nat. Acad. Sci., Washington, 1980; Evans, J. *Plantation Forestry in the Tropics*. Clarendon Press, Oxford, 1982.
2. Janzen, D. H. *The Ecology of Plants in the Tropics*. Arnold, London, 1975.
3. Goodland, R. J. A. and Irwin, R. S. *Landscape planning* **1** (1975), 123–254.
4. *Newsweek*, 25 Jan. 1982.
5. Whitmore, T. C. *Tropical Rain Forests of the Far East*. Clarendon Press, Oxford, 1975.
6. Melville, R. *Bull. Misc. Inf. Kew* **1936** (1936), 193–210; **1937** (1937), 274–276.
7. Ewel, J. (ed.) Tropical succession. *Biotropica* **12** (2) (Suppl), 1980.
8. Grainger, A. *The Ecologist* **10** (1980), 1–54.
9. Uhl, C. *et al. Oikos* **38** (1982), 313–320.
10. Opler, P. A. *et al.*, in Cairns, J. *et al.* (eds.) *Recovery and Restoration of Damaged Ecosystems*. Univ. Press Virginia, Charlottesville, 1977, pp. 379–421.
11. Fournier, P., in *Tropical Forest Ecosystems*, UNESCO, Paris, 1978, pp. 256–269.
12. Harcombe, P. *Ecology* **58** (1977), 1375–1383.
13. Nicholson, S. A. *Biotropica* **15** (1981), 110–116.
14. Ng, F. S. P. *Symposium—The Tropical Rain Forest*. Abstracts. Leeds, 1982.
15. Lugo, A. E. and Brown, S. *Unasylva* **32**, n. 129 (1980), 8–13.

16. Myers, N., in Synge, H. (ed.), *The Biological Aspects of Rare Plant Conservation*. Wiley, London, 1981, pp. 141–154.
17. Lovejoy, T., *Symposium—The Tropical Rain Forest*. Abstracts. Leeds, 1982.
18. Jacobs, M. *Fl. Males. Bull.* **35** (1982), 3768–3782.
19. Hall, J. B. and Swaine, M. D. *Distribution and Ecology of Vascular Plants in a Tropical Rain Forest*. Junk, The Hague, etc., 1981.
20. Poore, M. E. D. *New Phytol.* **90** (1982), 404–416.
21. Harley, J. L. *Proc. Roy. Soc. Lond.* (B) **197** (1977), 3–10.

Postscript (pp. 135–138)
1. Church, A. H. *Oxf. bot. Mem.* **13** (1922), repr. in D. J. Mabberley (ed.), *Revolutionary Botany*. Clarendon Press, Oxford, 1981, pp. 133–235.
2. Styles, B. T. and Vosa, C. G. *Taxon* **20** (1971), 485–499.
3. van Steenis, C. G. G. J. *Rheophytes of the World*, Sijthoff & Noordhoff, Alphen aan den Rijn, 1981, pp. 98–142.
4. White, F. *Mitt. bot. Staatsamml. München* **10** (1971), 91–112.
5. Kortlandt, A. *Symposium—The Tropical Rain Forest*. Poster Abstracts. Leeds, 1982.
6. Ashton, P. S. in *Tropical Forest Ecosystems*. UNESCO, Paris, 1978, pp. 180–215.
7. Ng, F. S. P. *Malays. For.* **40** (1977) 126–137.
8. Poore, M. E. D. *New Phytol.* **90** (1982), 404–416.
9. Corner, E. J. H. *New Phytol.* **45** (1946), 185–192.
10. Heywood, V. H. *Gdns' Bull., Sing.* **29** (1977), 233–237.

Index

The man who publishes a book without an index ought to be damned ten miles beyond hell, where the Devil himself cannot get for stinging nettles. (John Baynes, 1758–87).

145